ELECTIONS AND DEMOCRACY IN CENTRAL AMERICA, REVISITED

ELECTIONS AND DEMOCRACY IN CENTRAL AMERICA, REVISITED

NEW & ENLARGED EDITION

Edited by
Mitchell A. Seligson
John A. Booth

THE UNIVERSITY OF NORTH CAROLINA PRESS

Chapel Hill and London

To Susan Berk-Seligson & Patricia Bayer Richard

CONTENTS

PREFACE

This volume represents a continuation and significant expansion of the study of the relationship of elections to democracy in Central America that the editors began with *Elections and Democracy in Central America* (1989). It revisits the topic but goes considerably beyond what would normally constitute a mere second edition or updated version in several ways. First, all the country study chapters in Part 1 are wholly new and updated—many by new contributors. Second, we have added a section of topical chapters in Part 2 that explore themes and issues not treated systematically in the 1989 volume—comparative voting behavior, election observation, and the roles of external actors and of elites. Among the most notable innovations included in this volume is the use in several chapters of survey research materials on public opinion, electoral behavior, and political culture. The volume also benefits from an additional six years of Central American political and electoral history, a period marked by the invasion and installation by the United States of an elected regime in Panama in 1989, the electoral defeat of the Sandinista revolution in Nicaragua in 1990, the definitive end of both the Nicaraguan contra war and the Salvadoran insurrection, the full participation of El Salvador's former revolutionary party in the 1994 elections, and several other elections and regime changes. These developments provide our contributors and students of democratization and of the checkered politics of the Mesoamerican isthmus much new grist for the analytical mill.

We extend our warm thanks to Ken Coleman and Mike Dodson for their valuable comments on the manuscript. We acknowledge the support and encouragement of our departments and universities. We also thank the Latin American Studies Association for accepting the symposium entitled "Elections and Democracy in Central America," which was presented at the Seventeenth International Congress in Los Angeles in September 1992 and provided the first reading for the papers that constitute most of the volume.

The editors have, for more than two decades, enjoyed a frequent, produc-

ELECTIONS AND DEMOCRACY IN CENTRAL AMERICA, REVISITED

INTRODUCTION.
ELECTIONS AND DEMOCRACY
IN CENTRAL AMERICA: A
FRAMEWORK FOR ANALYSIS

John A. Booth

Many observers regarded Marco Vinicio Cerezo Arévalo's assumption of the presidency of Guatemala in January 1986 as a signal moment in the history of Central America because that event simultaneously gave five of the six main nations of the isthmus elected governments for the first time in memory.[1] By the mid-1990s all five of those elected governments had at least once peacefully transferred power to an opponent after losing an election. Moreover, in December 1989, a government that had been elected but fraudulently denied office in Panama a few months earlier was installed by force of a U.S. invasion and ouster of strongman Manuel Antonio Noriega.

Cautiously hopeful about the continuation of democracy in the isthmus but aware of its frailties,[2] observers of Central America were disappointed but hardly surprised by the coup attempted by Guatemalan president Jorge Serrano Elías on May 24, 1993. After minor protests of economic stagnation and government austerity policies, Serrano acted with at least partial military acquiescence when he dismissed the Guatemalan Congress and Supreme Court, established press censorship, and announced his intention to rule by decree. In a stunning reversal, however, protests by citizens, interest groups, political parties, the United States, the Organization of American States, and other external actors undermined the incipient dictatorship. After the Guatemalan Electoral Tribunal refused to call an election for a constituent assembly and the nation's Supreme Court decreed Serrano's actions illegal, the armed forces withdrew their support and forced him to resign on June 1, 1993.[3] Guatemala's Congress replaced Serrano with former human rights ombudsman Ramiro de León Carpio. Civilian government and constitutional order

port for elections in Central America but shifted in the Nicaraguan case from emphasizing military force to a policy of manipulating the 1990 election in order to end Sandinista rule (LASA 1990; Robinson 1992).

The remarkable prevalence and persistence of so many elected regimes in Central America and the flurry of sometimes contradictory actions by outside forces—all in the name of democracy—require serious scholarly study. This volume continues our efforts in this regard, constituting an expanded collection of all new studies of elections in Central American regimes.[5] Opinions diverge widely among policy makers, political theorists, and students of politics, however, about the essence of democracy and the role of elections in democratic governance and about how transitions to democracy occur. Key issues we must consider, then, are what constitutes political democracy and what elections have to do with building and maintaining democracy.

The Problem of Defining Democracy

One problem with the relationship of elections to democracy is a chronic imprecision of terminology. Political scientists either sloppily or conflictingly define and use the term *democracy* almost as frequently as politicians distort its meaning for political purposes. It is helpful to illustrate three common misuses of the word *democracy* before attempting to define it more precisely.

First, the term *democracy* often carries with it immense amounts of ideological freight. In the usage of politicians, ideologues, the media, and even scholars the word has become so broad as to be virtually meaningless. Such political distortions may badly obscure the meaning of particular elections and their possible contribution to democracy in Central America. For instance, the 1982 and 1984 Salvadoran elections were always described by the U.S. government as very "democratic," even though others regarded them as deeply flawed (Herman and Brodhead 1984, 93–153). Similarly, some observers contend that Nicaragua's 1984 election consolidated democracy there, whereas others treated it as transparently fraudulent. Such dissonance is hardly surprising given Central America's history of manipulated elections and given recent ideological and geopolitical conflict over the region.

Second, the virtual equation of democracy with elections is a posture that became common in post–World War II political science in the United States. Schumpeter (1943), Berelson (1954), Dahl (1956), and Lipset (1963), among others, have argued that allegedly inherent tendencies of mass publics to be authoritarian, irrational, antidemocratic, intolerant of civil liberties, and ill

Classical Definitions

The pluralist-elitist conception of democracy has been sharply criticized as too narrow by Bachrach (1966), Pateman (1970), and Mueller (1992), who charge that the pluralist-elitist approach distorts the original meaning and assumptions of the term *democracy*. "Classical" democratic theorists, who have had a clearer vision of democracy than most of the approaches just mentioned, may offer us a way out of this definitional thicket.[10]

Theorists over three millennia have identified the main characteristics of democratic governance. The key elements may be discerned quickly in the root of the word itself: *demos* means the people, *kratein* means to rule—rule by the people. Until obfuscation by the pluralist-elitist revisionists in the wake of World War II, the essential characteristic of democracy had generally been defined as the participation in rule of a society by its general populace. One convenient formulation of this idea treats democracy as *participation by the mass of people in a community in its governance (the making and carrying out of decisions)*. Political participation lies at the heart of democracy (Pateman 1970, 1–44). Such participation generally has been viewed as requiring equality of the right to participate for all sane, noncriminal adults.

Aristotle, for example, defined democracy as that constitution in which those who are both poor and free form a sovereign majority and therefore exercise some decision-making power in ruling and in judging disputes (Aristotle 1962, 74–81). Thomas Jefferson described the version of democracy that he most preferred as a "government by its citizens in mass, acting directly and personally, according to rules established by the majority" (Jefferson 1935, 83). John Stuart Mill described the "ideally best form of government" as one in which every citizen is, "at least occasionally, called on to take an actual part in the government by the personal discharge of some public function, local or general" (Mill 1958, 42).

The classical theorists of democracy strongly emphasized that participation educates the citizenry. Mill, for example, argued that "among the foremost benefits of free government is that education of the intelligence and of the sentiments which is carried down to the very lowest ranks of the people when they are called on to take a part in acts which directly affect the great interests of their country" (Mill 1958, 128). The political ability and civic values of the individual citizen are believed to develop through participation in politics. Similarly, political involvement breeds a political culture more amenable to democracy and more attentive to the collective good.

The classical approach to democracy has several implications. First, democracy involves public participation in decision making and administration,

governance, in order to conserve the most democracy "the powers of government, being divided, should be exercised each by representatives" (Jefferson 1935, 83). There is a necessary loss in the breadth of democracy, however, when a small number of representatives and administrative specialists make and carry out decisions on behalf of the mass of citizens. There is a necessary loss in the depth of democracy when citizens must delegate to leaders the determination of public decisions instead of making decisions as a whole. Depth of democracy is also sacrificed when political parties and other elites mediate between specialized institutions of representative government and the mass of citizens by selecting candidates for public office and setting the agendas and terms of public debate.

The classical approach would treat popular participation in leader selection through elections as one important aspect of democracy (one facet of participation in rule) but not its entire extent. The classical approach also views political participation—whether in elections or in other arenas—as educative, helping to develop individual talents and democratic values and to strengthen democracy. In contrast, the narrower, electoral focus of pluralist-elitists regards mass participation in arenas other than elections as either unimportant or even problematic. This school views mass publics as authoritarian, intolerant, and incompetent, so that participation by the majority of citizens in decision making, petitioning government, administration, and adjudication becomes potentially dangerous to constitutional electoral regimes. The educative aspects of citizen participation are largely ignored by the pluralist-elitists.

For the purposes of discussion in this chapter, democracy will be treated in the broader, classical sense of popular participation in rule, rather than the narrower, electoral focus associated with the position of the pluralist-elitists.

Rights and Democracy

Certain rights are essential to democracy. The most obvious and important, regardless of the type of political system, is the right to participate in public decisions. Citizens must have the effective freedom to participate in leadership choice (candidate selection and elections), policy decisions, and the implementation of decisions. Second, it follows that the principal condition under which the rights of one individual to participate in rule might be limited should be only to protect the fundamental right of other citizens to so participate.[11] Third, a constitution, an agreed-on contract among citizens specifying the rules for political intercourse, is of fundamental importance to protect citizens' rights. To promote democracy, a constitution must establish

require that contending forces have similar programs or visions of society. Such consensus is founded on a historic compromise among major political actors and social forces." In or around a democratizing election such a regime is forged, largely among important minorities (key political and economic elites) in the polity, when they agree to tolerate and accommodate one another. The forging of a regime among political and economic elites requires them to embrace and thereafter play by a set of rules of the game that include respect for legitimate competitors' rights, acceptance of a certain amount of mass involvement in politics, a definition of the role of the state, and agreement on means for resolution of conflict. The specific type of electoral system adopted may affect the prospects for the stability of the regime (Nohlen 1987, 17–41).

Because a truly democratizing election itself is only one small aspect of the forging of a regime, Karl (1986, 9) stresses that "elections themselves do not constitute democracy" and may actually impede the creation of a regime if unfairly manipulated or if imposed by forces from outside a society. Arguing along similar lines, Herman and Brodhead (1984, 5) see externally manipulated elections as barriers to democratization. They define "demonstration elections" as "organized and staged by a foreign power primarily to pacify its own restive home population, reassuring it that ongoing interventionary processes are legitimate and appreciated by their foreign objects." Their demonstration election concept can be extended to include elections held not under the aegis of an external power but staged by a government for its own symbolic purposes (Booth 1986, 38–40). Both externally and internally managed demonstration elections would typically lack freedoms to organize, to campaign and speak freely, and to vote without coercion. An election may also "liberalize" without democratizing. That is, an authoritarian regime may relax its usual repression during an election for the purpose of legitimizing itself or refurbishing its image but without truly adopting lasting participatory norms (Middlebrook 1986; Drake and Silva 1986a, 1986b; Dillon Soares 1986; Cornelius 1986).

Political Culture

Political culture has long been portrayed as evolving only gradually (Inglehart 1988, 1990), and there has been considerable skepticism about the general support of Latin Americans for democratic norms (Wiarda 1974, 1990; Fitzgibbon and Fernández 1981). Single elections in themselves seem unlikely to bring about dramatic changes in support for democracy (Paz 1985, 20).

However, the extent to which elections build, nurture, or consolidate a

significant opportunity for protecting one's self-interest or for promoting one's political goals.

Despite their potential to increase the array of participatory opportunities, however, elections and partisan activity constitute but a fraction of the political activity of any nation. The actual making of policy decisions, the execution of those decisions, and the adjudication of disputes involve vast arenas of ongoing public activity. In most countries, elections, party activity, and voting—even if highly efficacious—influence these arenas only tangentially, if at all. In some nations, the possibility of citizen initiative and referendum elections for making public decisions offers the public greater opportunities to decide policy matters directly (Magleby 1984; Barber 1974), but such practices are relatively rare in Latin America. There have been two recent but highly unusual opportunities for Central Americans to take direct part in framing fundamental laws. In 1985 and 1986 Nicaraguans contributed, especially through interest groups and citizens' forums, to the drafting of the new constitution adopted in early 1987. In November 1992 Panamanians, in a national referendum, voted down all sections of a proposed new constitution.[14]

2. What is the effect of the election(s) on the breadth of participation?

The breadth of participation (fraction of the citizenry participating) in elections is typically broadest for the actual casting of the ballot, with rates of up to three-quarters of those eligible voting in national elections common in many countries. Participation is customarily much narrower for campaigning and partisan activism (usually less than a quarter of the populace). Because citizens who have been forced to participate in consistently manipulated or fraudulent elections often become very inactive in politics, introducing open campaigns and fair elections can encourage a large increase in electoral participation and therefore broaden democracy, at least temporarily.[15]

It should be noted, however, that many other forms of political participation—voluntary group activity, contacting public officials, discussing public affairs—may involve more of the populace more of the time than most forms of electoral participation. Citizen involvement in such other, nonelectoral activities may not be significantly altered by the presence or absence of elections; they appear to go on in many types of regimes. It should also be noted that, with few exceptions, citizen participation in formal governmental arenas tends to be consistently higher among those who are more prosperous and better educated than it is among the poorer, less educated citizenry. Overall, then, elections and campaigns may broaden citizen political participation substantially but only within certain arenas, only for certain social strata, and typically only for limited periods.

- free and equal opportunity to register to vote
- free and equal opportunity to vote
- ballot secrecy, including the right to deposit secretly a null or blank ballot
- freedom from intimidation or coercion as to how to vote
- equal weight of the counted vote

To ensure these conditions for individual citizens requires other structural and contextual conditions for the polity as a whole:

- freedom for parties to organize, electioneer, campaign, and distribute propaganda
- absence of an unfair advantage by particular minorities, especially for incumbents in office
- mechanisms to adjudicate and redress grievances among contenders
- fair and free systems of registration and election administration, and a true count of the votes
- respect for the winners' right to rule by the losers; respect for the losers' and other minorities' right to continued participation

The evaluation of such conditions by observers and participants is a fairly straightforward matter in an open electoral environment. There has arisen in Central America and Latin America overall a small legal-scholarly-technical industry that studies, advises on, and promotes fair elections, including the Association of Electoral Organizations of Central America and the Caribbean and the Inter-American Center for Electoral Advice and Promotion, a subsidiary of the Inter-American Court of Human Rights. Many human rights and special interest organizations monitor and observe elections in Central America, including the Council of Freely Elected Heads of Government, represented by former U.S. president Jimmy Carter in Panama's 1989 election and Nicaragua's 1990 balloting. Perhaps even more significant is the recent involvement of intergovernmental organizations such as the Organization of American States and the United Nations in monitoring elections, most notably in Nicaragua in 1990 and in El Salvador in 1994. This large-scale international organizational presence grew out of the Central American Peace Accord, signed by five Central American presidents in 1987, and subsequent regional summit agreements, in which Costa Rica, Guatemala, El Salvador, Honduras, and Nicaragua in effect invited outside monitoring to assure the quality of certain elections.

External involvement in elections may go beyond merely bearing impartial witness and lose its impartiality in pursuit of narrow partisan, ideological, or geopolitical interests. As Moreno reveals in his chapter, U.S. involvement in

The consolidation of Venezuela's democratic regime took longer and was more tenuous. After sectarian conflict undermined an interlude of civilian rule in the late 1940s, Venezuela's three major parties reached an accord in the late 1950s to play by liberal democratic rules if the dictator Pérez Jiménez could be toppled. Support for the liberal regime by the national bourgeoisie developed slowly in Venezuela, and forbearance from intervention by the armed forces was tenuous at first.

In Central America three cases of possible regime consolidation bear further scrutiny. In Nicaragua in 1990 the Sandinistas, defeated at the ballot box by the United Nicaraguan Opposition (Unión Nicaragüense Opositora—UNO) coalition, transferred power to Violeta Barrios de Chamorro. This process involved a series of accords to facilitate transition and help demobilize the contras. Despite such agreements, several years later the new Nicaraguan government appeared highly unstable and hamstrung by severe internal divisions and resurgent political violence. In El Salvador the peace negotiations between the Nationalist Republican Alliance (Alianza Republicana Nacionalista—ARENA) government of President Alfredo Cristiani and the rebel Farabundo Martí National Liberation Front (Frente Farabundo Martí para la Liberación Nacional—FMLN) finally ended in an accord in January 1992. In contrast to Nicaragua, a more successful interelite accord seemed to have been struck and, if it holds, may constitute the base of a new electoral regime in El Salvador. In Guatemala, President Serrano's dramatic power grab of May 1993 revealed his lack of commitment to democratic rules even though he was an elected leader. That Serrano failed because of protests by major political forces revealed a widening consensus among Guatemalan political elites in favor of democratic rules. Equivocation by the army and other actors, however, indicated major obstacles to an inclusive democratic interelite settlement (Golden 1993g).

6. Did the election(s) contribute to a political culture of support for participation and for democratic rules?

The growth of elite and popular support for participatory politics and for democratic rules and liberties is likely to be fitful and to require the passage of many years, if not decades. Indeed, some commentators argue that Latin American political culture begins from historical roots in Catholic Spain and has been so shaped by centuries of political history that the region's culture is generally antithetical to democratic beliefs. Others have argued that these traditions have recently led major Latin American elite and middle-sector groups to forge antidemocratic alliances with military authoritarians in defense of their class interests (Wiarda 1974; O'Donnell 1979). Despite such

Notes

1. "Central America," by colonial and national historical traditions and international integration arrangements, traditionally has included only five of the seven nations of the Mesoamerican isthmus—Guatemala, Honduras, El Salvador, Nicaragua, and Costa Rica. Although geographically on the isthmus, Panama was part of Colombia until 1903. Because of its increasing integration into Hispanic Mesoamerica and the dramatic political events there since the first edition of this volume was published, we have included Panama. We exclude Belize because of its cultural and geopolitical distinctness.

2. The absence of many factors that contribute to the consolidation of democracy made Guatemala appear a high risk for democratic failure (Booth 1993).

3. See Golden (1993a, 1993b, 1993c, 1993d, 1993e, 1993f, 1993g).

4. This includes several elections in El Salvador in the 1980s, in Nicaragua in 1984 and 1990, Panama in 1989, and Guatemala in 1985 and 1990–91.

5. See our *Elections and Democracy in Central America* (1989); the present anthology adds the Panamanian case and chapters on elites, election observation, external actors, and comparative voting behavior. See also Goodman et al. (1992) for an examination of the role of parties in democratization.

6. Macpherson (1966, 1977) traces liberalism through various stages—protective (or Lockean) democracy, developmental democracy, and equilibrium (pluralist) democracy—and contrasts them with other variants. Cohen (1982) identifies individualist and socialist democracies but describes communism as nondemocratic. Przeworski (1986) describes social democracy as a liberal constitutional regime that would reform rather than replace capitalism, as would revolutionary socialism. Lijphart (1984) has studied both consociational democracies in plural societies and twenty-one constitutional, electoral governments. In another study Lijphart (1977) examines majoritarian and consensus democracies. Yates (1982) describes the modern U.S. system as a bureaucratic democracy.

7. One subset of this literature focuses on the role of external actors, especially the United States, in promoting transition to democracy in Latin America. See, for instance, Lowenthal (1991), Pastor (1989), and Carothers (1991).

8. The first edition of this volume (Booth and Seligson 1989) examined the potential contribution of elections to democratization in Central America and found the prospects for consolidating democracy mixed at best.

9. For other studies using this approach, see, for instance, Roy (1992), Barba Solano et al. (1991), and Domínguez and Lindenberg (1993).

10. Pateman (1970) notes that "classical democratic theory" is a somewhat inaccurate designation because the theories she includes in the category span three millennia from Aristotle to J. S. Mill. I am using the term *classical* very loosely here, as did she, for the sake of convenience.

11. This provision notwithstanding, almost all democratic models exclude from participation persons incapacitated by youth, lunacy, or criminality.

12. See also Rosenberg (1985, 23–33).

13. I am using the term *democratizing* as Paul Drake and Eduardo Silva do in "Introduction: Elections and Democratization in Latin America, 1980–1985" (1986a, 2–3), rather than as Petras (1986, 1–15) and Rabine (1986, 59–64) do. The latter approach suggests that the election of civilian regimes in Latin America can mean nothing more than a more effective mechanism by which an old regime continues to exploit the poor and block popular democracy. I would argue that if such occurred, no true "democratization" as intended here would have taken place.

the Conference on Deepening Democracy and Representation in Latin America, University of Pittsburgh, April 17–18.

Booth, John A., and Mitchell A. Seligson. 1984. "The Political Culture of Authoritarianism in Mexico: A Reexamination." *Latin American Research Review* 19, no. 1:106–24.

———. 1993. "Paths to Democracy and the Political Culture of Costa Rica, Mexico, and Nicaragua." In *Political Culture and Democracy in Developing Countries*, edited by Larry Diamond, 107–39. Boulder, Colo.: Lynne Rienner.

———, eds. 1989. *Elections and Democracy in Central America*. Chapel Hill: University of North Carolina Press.

Carothers, Thomas. 1991. *In the Name of Democracy: U.S. Policy toward Latin America in the Reagan Years*. Berkeley and Los Angeles: University of California Press.

Carvajal Herrera, Mario. 1978. *Actitudes políticas del costarricense*. San José, Costa Rica: Editorial Costa Rica.

Cohen, Carl. 1971. *Democracy*. New York: Free Press.

———. 1982. *Four Systems*. New York: Random House.

Contemporary Marxism. 1986. Vol. 14 (Fall), special issue on Latin America.

Cornelius, Wayne A. 1986. "Political Liberalization and the 1985 Elections in Mexico." In *Elections and Democratization in Latin America, 1980–1985*, edited by Paul W. Drake and Eduardo Silva, 115–42. La Jolla: Center for Iberian and Latin American Studies and Center for U.S.-Mexican Studies, University of California at San Diego.

Dahl, Robert A. 1956. *A Preface to Democratic Theory*. Chicago: University of Chicago Press.

———. 1971. *Polyarchy*. New Haven: Yale University Press.

Diamond, Larry. 1993a. "Introduction: Political Culture and Democracy." In *Political Culture and Democracy in Developing Countries*, edited by Larry Diamond, 1–34. Boulder, Colo.: Lynne Rienner.

———, ed. 1993b. *Political Culture and Democracy in Developing Countries*. Boulder, Colo.: Lynne Rienner.

Diamond, Larry, Juan J. Linz, and Seymour Martin Lipset, eds. 1989. *Democracy in Developing Countries: Latin America*. Boulder, Colo.: Lynne Rienner.

Dillon Soares, Glaucio Ary. 1986. "Elections and the Redemocratization of Brazil." In *Elections and Democratization in Latin America, 1980–1985*, edited by Paul W. Drake and Eduardo Silva, 273–98. La Jolla: Center for Iberian and Latin American Studies and Center for U.S.-Mexican Studies, University of California at San Diego.

Domínguez, Jorge I., and Marc Lindenberg, eds. 1993. *Democratic Transitions in Central America and Panama*. Boston: World Peace Foundation.

Drake, Paul W., and Eduardo Silva. 1986a. Introduction to *Elections and Democratization in Latin America, 1980–1985*, edited by Paul W. Drake and Eduardo Silva, 1–8. La Jolla: Center for Iberian and Latin American Studies and Center for U.S.-Mexican Studies, University of California at San Diego.

———, eds. 1986b. *Elections and Democratization in Latin America, 1980–1985*. La Jolla: Center for Iberian and Latin American Studies and Center for U.S.-Mexican Studies, University of California at San Diego.

Fitzgibbon, R. H., and J. A. Fernández, eds. 1981. *Latin America: Political Culture and Development*. Englewood Cliffs, N.J.: Prentice-Hall.

García Laguardia, Jorge Mario. 1986. Prólogo to *Legislación electoral comparada: Colombia, México, Panamá, Venezuela, y Centroamérica*, edited by Cecilia Cortés, 7–11. San José, Costa Rica: Centro de Asesoría y Promoción Electoral–Instituto Interamericano de Derechos Humanos/Instituto de Investigaciones Jurídicas–Universidad Nacional Autónoma de México.

Golden, Tim. 1993a. "Guatemalans Protest the President's Power Grab." *New York Times*, May 27, A4.

———. 1993b. "Guatemalan's Power Grab Brings Street Protests." *New York Times*, May 28, A5.

———. 1993c. "Central Americans Turn Once More to the Army." *New York Times*, May 30, sec. 4, p. 6.

———. 1993d. "Pressure Mounting on Guatemalan in Power Grab." *New York Times*, May 31, A5.

———. 1993e. "Guatemalan Who Grabbed Power Is Out." *New York Times*, June 2, A6.

———. 1993f. "Army Role Hinted as Guatemala Writhes Again." *New York Times*, June 4, A5.

Nohlen, Dieter. 1987. *La reforma electoral en América Latina: Seis contribuciones al debate*. San José, Costa Rica: Instituto Interamericano de Derechos Humanos–Centro Interamericano de Asesoría y Promoción Electoral.

O'Donnell, Guillermo. 1979. *Modernization and Bureaucratic Authoritarianism*. Berkeley: Institute of International Studies, University of California.

O'Donnell, Guillermo, Philippe Schmitter, and Laurence Whitehead, eds. 1986. *Transitions from Authoritarian Rule*. Baltimore: Johns Hopkins University Press.

Packenham, Robert A. 1992. *The Dependency Movement: Scholarship and Politics in Development Studies*. Cambridge: Harvard University Press.

Pastor, Robert A. 1989. *Democracy in the Americas: Stopping the Pendulum*. New York: Holmes and Meier.

Pateman, Carole. 1970. *Participation and Democratic Theory*. Cambridge: Cambridge University Press.

Paz, Octavio. 1985. "La democracia en América Latina." In *Frustraciones de un destino: La democracia en América Latina*, by Octavio Paz, Carlos Rangel, Jean Meyer, Enrique Krauze, Gabriel Zaid, Carlos Franqui, Guillermo Cabrera Infante, and Rodolfo Pastor, 11–36. San José, Costa Rica: Libro Libre.

Peeler, John. 1985. *Latin American Democracies: Colombia, Costa Rica, Venezuela*. Chapel Hill: University of North Carolina Press.

Petras, James. 1986. "The Redemocratization Process." *Contemporary Marxism* 14 (Fall): 1–15.

Przeworski, Adam. 1986. *Capitalism and Social Democracy*. Cambridge: Harvard University Press.

Rabine, Mark. 1986. "Guatemala: 'Redemocratization' or Civilian Counterinsurgency?" *Contemporary Marxism* 14 (Fall): 59–64.

Reuschemeyer, Dietrich, Evelyne Huber Stephens, and John D. Stephens. 1992. *Capitalist Development and Democracy*. Chicago: University of Chicago Press.

Robinson, William I. 1992. *The Faustian Bargain: U.S. Involvement in Nicaraguan Elections, U.S. Foreign Policy in the Post–Cold War Era*. Boulder, Colo.: Westview Press.

Rosenberg, Mark. 1985. *¿Democracia en Centroamérica?* Cuadernos de CAPEL, no. 5. San José, Costa Rica: Instituto Interamericano de Derechos Humanos–Centro de Asesoría y Promoción Electoral.

Roy, Joaquín, ed. 1992. *The Reconstruction of Central America: The Role of the European Community*. Coral Gables, Fla.: Iberian Studies Institute–European Community Research Institute, University of Miami.

Schumpeter, Joseph A. 1943. *Capitalism, Socialism, and Democracy*. London: Allen and Unwin.

Seligson, Mitchell A., and John A. Booth. 1993. "Political Culture and Regime Type: Some Evidence from Nicaragua and Costa Rica." *Journal of Politics* 55 (August): 777–92.

Seligson, Mitchell A., and Miguel Gómez B. 1989. "Ordinary Elections in Extraordinary Times: The Political Economy of Voting in Costa Rica." In *Elections and Democracy in Central America*, edited by John A. Booth and Mitchell A. Seligson, 158–84. Chapel Hill: University of North Carolina Press.

Sisson, Richard. 1993. "Culture and Democratization in India." In *Political Culture and Democracy in Developing Countries*, edited by Larry Diamond, 37–65. Boulder, Colo.: Lynne Rienner.

U.S. Department of State. 1987. *Democracy in Latin America and the Caribbean: The Promise and the Challenge*. Washington, D.C.: Bureau of Public Affairs (March).

Vanhanen, Tatu. 1990. *The Process of Democratization: A Comparative Study of 147 States, 1980–1988*. New York: Crane Russak.

———. 1992a. "Social Constraints of Democratization." In *Strategies of Democratization*, edited by Tatu Vanhanen, 19–35. Washington, D.C.: Crane Russak.

———, ed. 1992b. *Strategies of Democratization*. Washington, D.C.: Crane Russak.

Wiarda, Howard J. 1990. *The Democratic Revolution in Latin America: History, Politics, and U.S. Policy*. New York: Holmes and Meier.

———, ed. 1974. *Politics and Social Change in Latin America: The Distinct Tradition*. Amherst: University of Massachusetts Press.

Yates, Douglas. 1982. *Bureaucratic Democracy*. Cambridge: Harvard University Press.

PART ONE:
COUNTRY STUDIES

1

ELECTORAL PROBLEMS AND THE DEMOCRATIC PROJECT IN GUATEMALA

Susanne Jonas

From a commonsense perspective, what does it mean to speak of "democratization" in Guatemala, where daily life for many people remains thoroughly militarized and repressive? And why focus on elections in an environment where electoral democracy has been severely restricted and is widely regarded as having discredited civilian rule? These questions seem especially pertinent at the moment when neighboring El Salvador, by contrast, has just held elections that at least included participation by former insurgents.

In the real world of Guatemala, elections since the mid-1980s have been meaningful only as one element—by no means the centerpiece—of a long-range democratizing project. Their legacy should be interpreted in conjunction with initiatives by other actors, in the informal nonelectoral arenas of politics, to open up an exclusionary system and give reality to constitutional guarantees that exist on paper. One of the most important such initiatives, I argue, is the peace process to end the thirty-four-year civil war. In fact, recent experiences throughout Central America suggest that in countries emerging from decades of revolutionary struggle, democratization involves a complex interplay of such struggles and their resolution with the institutionalization of representative democracy. From this perspective, I propose a reformulation that goes beyond the critique of recent "top-down" elections, conducted within a framework of war and state-sponsored violence, to suggest under what conditions future electoral efforts could contribute more significantly to Guatemala's democratization.

Our starting point is the formulation of democracy adopted by Booth (1989, 11) and other analysts, "participation by the mass of people in a community in its governance." This presupposes a concept of citizenship in which the popu-

This succeeded in repressive terms but in no way represented a stable, lasting political project. By 1982 the divisions within the ruling coalition were serious enough to force the military to change the nature of its rule.

The change began during the height of the army's scorched earth war against the second wave of the revolutionary uprising, centered in the indigenous highlands—a war that between 1981 and 1983 alone, according to international organizations including the Organization of American States (OAS) Inter-American Commission on Human Rights as well as church sources, cost the lives of 100,000–150,000 civilians (mostly unarmed) and saw the destruction of 440 villages, by the army's own figures. Following the third successive electoral fraud in March 1982, General Efraín Ríos Montt staged a coup, which initiated a change in political objectives, once the most brutal phase of the counterinsurgency war had accomplished its goals. By August 1983, Ríos Montt had lost support from key sectors in the ruling coalition and was replaced in a second coup led by General Oscar Humberto Mejía Víctores. According to leading civilian participants (ASIES 1988; interviews), both governments had the same basic goals, that is, to begin a controlled return to civilian rule—in the army's own view, to conduct politics as a "continuation of war by other means," in order to regain the confidence of the bourgeoisie and the passive consent of other sectors of the population, and to annihilate the Left politically.

During this transition, electoral politics was revived, using the language of pluralism and national reconciliation and bringing in those political parties acceptable to the army. This extended to the Christian Democratic Party, which had for years attempted to develop an alliance with segments of the army. The army even took a risk on the fledgling Socialist Democratic Party (Partido Socialista Democrático—PSD) once it had accepted the rules of the game, renouncing any alliance with the insurgent Left. (In any case, many leading social democratic politicians had been assassinated during the 1970s.) Meanwhile, a significant proportion of the electorate remained effectively disenfranchised, lacking meaningful options, since all left parties were illegal.

The intellectual authors of this process, participants, and sympathetic observers argue that the coups of 1982 and 1983 actually began the process of redemocratization and normalization of Guatemalan politics (ASIES 1988; interviews). In fact, given the very restricted rules of the game, it was more a process of legitimating a slightly liberalized regime than of restoring true legitimacy.[3]

The first step was the June 1984 election for a constituent assembly, to draft a new constitution and electoral laws. The major participants were the traditional rightist parties (the ultrarightist National Liberation Movement [Movi-

election with high hopes, as a possible turning point—an opportunity to express their rejection of military dictatorship and their desire for democracy and reform. Those who voted gave a 70 percent mandate in the runoff election to Cerezo, who was the most progressive of the major candidates.

Although there are many shades of interpretation of the 1985 election,[4] most observers agree that, despite the democratic aspirations of a majority of Guatemalans, it did not effectively transfer power from the army to civilians. Although the balance between civilians and military did change in some respects after 1986, basic counterinsurgency institutions were legalized in the 1985 constitution, and in practice the army retained implicit veto powers in significant policy (and budgetary) areas. The army also granted itself amnesty for its previous crimes before turning over the government to Cerezo. For these reasons, the 1985 elections did not by themselves initiate a fundamental break from the counterinsurgency state, whose essence is best captured in Carlos Figueroa's image (1986) of the centaur-state, half man and half beast.

The Guatemalan army viewed the 1985 election as a new stage or adjustment in its counterinsurgency strategy. It preferred civilian rule in part because, after being an international pariah for many years, the government needed international legitimacy in order to obtain foreign aid to deal with the economic crisis. Even more important were internal pressures for the election. A more "open" political environment was seen as necessary in Guatemala, in order to regain private-sector confidence and reactivate the economy. Further, a civilian government might reestablish stability and limit social protest, hence addressing the political crisis. Even though the army had tactically and temporarily defeated the guerrillas in the early 1980s, it was discredited after years of fraudulent rule; it sought to redefine its relations with the population, in part by taking credit for returning the country to civilian rule.

Recognizing the political crisis, the U.S. government also played an active role in the 1985 election process, providing funds both directly and indirectly, through the National Endowment for Democracy (NED). Reagan administration officials celebrated Guatemala as having completed its democratic transition—in part to use Guatemala as a counterexample to Sandinista Nicaragua, whose 1984 election the United States never accepted as legitimate.

Contradictions of the 1986–1990 Political Opening

Even with all the serious limitations of the 1983–85 political process, the return of civilian rule under a moderate government awakened profound

and boycotted at that time by the army, government, and private sector, the dialogue expressed a widening national consensus among other sectors in favor of a political settlement to the war. In 1990 the URNG held a series of meetings with the political parties and subsequently with the major social sectors, including the private business sector.

The dialogue process was significant because it began to open up spaces within a repressive context for public discussion of issues that had been taboo for decades, such as the causes of the war and possible constitutional reforms. It also permitted the gradual emergence of the URNG as a central player (even while illegal) in public debate. As will be seen, this affected the 1990–91 election and put pressure on the new government and the army to begin formal negotiations in 1991.

The Election of 1990–1991 and the Politics of Abstention

Throughout 1990 Guatemalans prepared for the November election, amid deepening economic crisis and increasing political violence. More generally, as noted by the National Democratic Institute for International Affairs (NDI; an offshoot of the U.S. government–funded NED), "the campaign environment did not allow for unfettered debate. . . . The violence constricted the political spectrum by discouraging participation in the political process and suppressing countervailing points of view" (NDI 1991, 59). The tensions of the electoral process itself generated new violence, including assassinations of a number of candidates. Various analysts directly linked the instability of the election period to the absence of serious options for the majority of the population. Among the thirteen candidates, there was not one center-left contender, a situation described by analyst José Luis Cruz Salazar (1991) as "fraudulent pluralism."

The Christian Democratic Party was divided, corrupt, and scandal ridden. Halfway through the election, it attempted to compensate for its weaknesses by shifting toward a more populist stance. Although the Right never managed to unify around one candidate, it always seemed most likely that the victor would be a New Rightist—the possibilities ranging from the UCN's more moderate Jorge Carpio to more extreme but "modern" MLN candidates, to conservative Protestant fundamentalist maverick Jorge Serrano Elías. Former dictator Ríos Montt campaigned as a candidate of law and order and garnered considerable support before his candidacy was finally barred on constitutional grounds.

None of these candidates addressed the issues of repression or impunity for human rights abusers. All were committed to neoliberal economic policies

made efforts to give the appearance of establishing civilian control the army, in part to stem the constant international criticisms of human rights violations. Serrano also understood that taking initiatives to negotiate with the URNG was one of his few hopes to establish legitimacy for his government.

But Serrano's government quickly began to be plagued by the accumulated contradictions of the top-down transition. By mid-1992, all branches of the government showed signs of a critical institutional crisis:[5]

- In the executive branch, nepotism, corruption, and drug-related scandals turned the cabinet into a virtual revolving door. By 1993 the president himself was directly implicated in making his personal fortune from the privatization of the electrical industry.

- At the same time, according to reports in the Guatemalan press, only 20 to 30 percent of the population believed in the efficacy of the judicial system, perceived as politicized, corrupt, and inefficacious.

- Congress degenerated into a miasma of influence peddling and corruption, including several serious drug-trafficking scandals. Moreover, the traditional political parties had managed to garner affiliation from only 4.34 percent of the adult population (Cuestas 1991, 32). They were oriented purely toward winning elections rather than channeling popular demands or generating consensus; they feared developing links to popular, indigenous, or human rights organizations because the latter were dubbed "subversive" by the army. The lack of representativity of the parties was directly related to the low level of organization permitted in Guatemalan civil society overall (Poitevín 1992, 28–29).

- Most serious as a threat to democracy and legitimacy was the army's continuing impunity for human rights crimes, which had not been resolved by the return to nominal civilian rule. Serrano's ability to maintain civilian control over the military diminished, and his policy decisions increasingly reflected the army's priorities. Hence, there persisted a generalized perception that the practices of past military dictatorships were continuing (Cuestas 1992, 14) and that Guatemala still did not effectively enjoy the rule of law.

- Under pressure from many quarters, Serrano opened formal peace negotiations with the URNG in April 1991. But after initial agreements in principle on democratization and partial agreements on human rights in 1991 and 1992, Serrano subsequently attempted to dictate further terms of peace unilaterally. By May 1993 the peace talks had broken down.

The "Serranazo" of May–June 1993: Transition by Implosion

In the early morning hours of May 25, 1993, President Serrano, initially with support from hard-line sectors of the army high command, staged an *auto-golpe* (self-coup), suspending sections of the constitution and dissolving Congress and the Supreme Court. This move was a response to multiple conjunctural factors: Serrano's growing political isolation; his confrontation with Congress over his corrupt business deals; increasing popular discontent and mobilizations against neoliberal austerity measures; and the breakdown of the peace negotiations in early May. At a deeper level, the coup was a response to the accumulation of structural crises that had made Guatemala increasingly ungovernable. The contradictions of the top-down transition since 1982 had made the system far too brittle to withstand the force of rising demands for change.

From the first moment, public opposition to the coup was clear. Resistance by the organized forces of civil society, combined with strong international pressures, turned even Serrano's allies in the private sector and the army against him (and a week later, against his rightist vice president, who attempted to take power). As a sign of which way the winds were blowing, the army did not go into the streets to suppress protests. Diverse currents of public opinion came together in new forums such as the Instancia Nacional de Consenso (National Instance of Consensus), a broad alliance of civilian sectors ranging from the business community to popular organizations, and the Foro Multisectorial Social (Multisectoral Social Forum), a new coalition of popular organizations. Throughout the crisis, the Constitutional Court, and to a lesser extent the Supreme Electoral Tribunal, played a central role in defining a legal road out of the crisis and returning the country to a constitutional order. The succession was ultimately resolved on June 5, when Congress elected Serrano's erstwhile enemy, Human Rights Ombudsman Ramiro de León Carpio, as president.

What produced this improbable outcome? Internally, three factors stand out. First, after decades of extreme political polarization, Guatemala experienced one of those rare historical moments in which virtually all organized sectors of society (at least in the capital city) agreed to resist yet another violation of the constitutional order. Second, this broad consensus was strengthened by unusually strong international pressures, including threats from the United States and the European Community to suspend trade privileges, economic aid, and access to international credit. These pressures convinced waverers in the private sector to be "constitutionalist." Third, at key moments, tactical divisions surfaced within the army officer corps, so that army hard-

standoff between Congress and the president soon degenerated into daily turmoil and even physical confrontations among different factions. During October and November there were continual rumors of a suspension of constitutional liberties or even a coup. The Bishops' Council of the Catholic Church finally stepped in as mediator, and a compromise was reached in mid-November.

The complex settlement, to be voted up or down in a January 1994 referendum, called for reforms in the election of Congress and the Supreme Court, controls over congressional immunity as well as new congressional elections in mid-1994, shorter terms of office for both president and Congress, and elimination of confidential expenditures in Ministerial budgets—all of which were designed to reduce the level of corruption in public life. This compromise gained the political system a new lease on life but not lasting legitimacy. The January 1994 vote only underlined the continuing and massive crisis of the political system, as 84 percent of eligible voters abstained from voting in the referendum. Although de León Carpio's compromise package was approved, the astoundingly high abstention rate made clear that this could in no way be interpreted as a "mandate" for the government.

Democracy as Problem versus Democracy as Project

As of 1994, recent elections have not by themselves contributed meaningfully to expanding the range, breadth, or depth of political participation. In regard to range, these elections permitted discussion only of issues acceptable to the military and bourgeoisie (not, for example, land reform), and then only of certain acceptable positions on those issues. In regard to breadth, the unrepresentative quality of these elections reached its logical extreme in 1990–91, when more than two-thirds of the eligible electorate did not cast valid ballots. Finally, in regard to depth, these elections have not incorporated the excluded majority sectors of the population into the decision-making process. To the extent that those sectors are attempting to insert themselves or their agendas, it is primarily through extra-electoral struggles. Nevertheless, the return to institutional democracy has unquestionably enhanced the ability of the various forces in civil society to wage these struggles by creating some space for discussion and for the reemergence—albeit slow and costly—of popular organizations.

What might the future hold for Guatemala? The crises of 1993 made clear the fragility of the existing civilian order, and Guatemala in 1994 remained at a crossroads. Prospects for the near-term future remained ambiguous. Further

commission," as in El Salvador, to determine responsibility for past human rights crimes. Although almost certainly lacking the power to punish the past abusers, such a commission and its investigation could establish responsibility for their deeds and discourage continuing impunity. Peace seems also a precondition for electoral campaigns in which candidates will not have to make implicit prior deals with the army. Finally, the negotiations highlight the need for constitutional reforms (Ilom 1992, 7)—also being called for by indigenous and other organizations—to make existing institutions more representative and to permit new forms of political organization.

In short, a just peace is a precondition for changing the rules of the political game, ending the lingering cold-war polarization in Guatemala, and giving a truly democratic content to elections. In this sense, the peace process is the necessary complement to elections in Guatemala's democratic transition (as in El Salvador's). The consensus being constructed in this arena and in articulation with other initiatives originating in civil society—one reflection of which is the growing demand by popular and indigenous organizations to participate directly in the peace process—is much broader and more likely to bring lasting stability to Guatemala than the purely electoral (quite exclusionary) interelite pact of the mid-1980s that initiated the transition to civilian rule.[8]

In Guatemala, with its majority indigenous population, genuine pluralism also implies the construction of a multiethnic, multicultural nation and recognition of the strong indigenous component of Guatemala's identity. Discussions of indigenous rights, even autonomy, are arising not only in the peace process but also in numerous proposals for legal and constitutional reforms (beginning with approval of the International Labor Organization's Convenio 169). Indigenous movements are also inventing new forms of political organization; in the May 1993 municipal elections, they created their own *comités cívicos* (civic committees) in many towns, rather than choosing among the traditional political parties. These and other initiatives could profoundly enrich the content of Guatemala's democratic project by incorporating indigenous traditions of community democracy. (See Cojtí 1991; Poitevín 1991, 1992; Solares 1992; Bastos and Camus 1993.)

Finally, a word about socioeconomic aspects of democracy, which are closely related to (but not synonymous with) political democracy. Many Guatemalans argue that so long as nearly three-fourths of the population lives in extreme poverty, formal democracy will remain forever fragile. As Guatemalan analysts Poitevín (1992, 35–37) and Torres Rivas (1991a) argue, social struggles, which establish a material base for the exercise of rights as citizens, have become the condition for liberal democracy.[9]

4. Some Guatemalan analysts refer ironically to the contradictory experience of the 1985 election and rejection of military government as being perhaps Guatemala's "best hope" to begin a democratic transition. Others have referred to it as a *consulta pública* (consultation with the public), a controlled attempt at legitimation within the context of ongoing counterinsurgency war. Elsewhere the resulting government has been described as a "facade democracy," which combined formal legality with illegal violence and in which the army remained the fundamental source of power (interviews; Torres Rivas 1987; Aguilera 1986, 1985; Rosada 1986a; Solórzano 1987), or as "an authoritarian transition to democracy" (Torres Rivas 1989).

5. The following items were amply documented in the Guatemalan press, in analyses by various research institutes, and in wide-ranging interviews during 1992 and 1993.

6. Elsewhere (Jonas 1991, 172–74), I have developed more fully the argument that the Guatemalan counterinsurgency state is essentially a weak state. Hinkelammert (1994) argues more broadly that a strong state is one that foments the development of all sectors of civil society (not just the bourgeoisie).

7. A number of Guatemalans of various political orientations consider that the crisis of May could have had a very different outcome—a semirevolutionary rupture as in 1944, rather than a recomposition (preservation) of the system. One of the key players in saving the system subsequently observed that they may have "entrapped" themselves in legality. In a similar vein, others viewed the outcome as a lost opportunity for far-reaching change without bloodshed. In the heat of the crisis, the long-range stakes were perhaps obscured by the search for an immediate solution. At crucial moments, moreover, the improvised coalition of popular forces, although more united than ever before, was not strong enough to shape the outcome, leaving the initiative in the hands of more conservative domestic and international actors.

8. It is precisely the articulation between the peace negotiations and the empowerment, concurrently, of forces in civil society that differentiates this situation from (or requires a broader interpretation of) interelite accords (see Peeler 1992). Even if the definition of "elites" is applied to the URNG as a "counterelite," such an accord is a necessary but insufficient condition for overcoming the legacy of exclusionary politics in Guatemala—all the more so because of the particular claims of indigenous peoples that are coming to the forefront of Guatemalan politics.

9. I wish to emphasize two interrelated points here. First, as stated at the outset, the definition of political democracy underlying this chapter (and indeed this entire volume) is "popular participation in rule" (Booth 1989, 13); this goes beyond a strictly electoral definition of democracy and also beyond other "minimalist" formulations in which participation is not central to the definition. Second, without confusing political democracy with social equality definitionally, we can cite concrete experience over the past decade as demonstrating the necessity of the latter for consolidating the former in a stable, lasting manner. If a reminder is needed, we can find it in the recent coup attempts (directed primarily against austerity policies) in Venezuela, previously assumed to be a fully stable and consolidated democracy. For further discussion of the integral relation between representative and participatory democracy more generally (outside Central America, e.g., in the Southern Cone), see Nun (1991, 26–27), Weffort (1992, 31–32, 56), Borón (1993), and Touraine (1991). To put it another way, "integral democracy" implies a concern with human development and is inconsistent with what Peeler (1992, n. 20) calls "predatory class relations."

———. 1989. "Elections and Transitions: The Guatemalan and Nicaraguan Cases." In *Elections and Democracy in Central America*, edited by John A. Booth and Mitchell A. Seligson, 126–57. Chapel Hill: University of North Carolina Press.

———. 1991. *The Battle for Guatemala: Rebels, Death Squads, and U.S. Power*. Boulder, Colo.: Westview Press.

———. 1994. "Text and Subtext of the Guatemalan Political Drama." *LASA Forum*. Latin American Studies Association (LASA). (Winter): 3–9.

Jonas, Susanne, and Edward J. McCaughan, eds. 1994. *Latin America Faces the Twenty-first Century*. Boulder, Colo.: Westview Press.

Jonas, Susanne, and Nancy Stein, eds. 1990. *Democracy in Latin America: Visions and Realities*. New York: Bergin and Garvey.

Karl, Terry. 1990. "Dilemmas of Democratization in Latin America." *Comparative Politics* (October): 1–21.

Lowy, Michael, and Eder Sader. 1985. "The Militarization of the State in Latin America." *Latin American Perspectives* (Fall): 7–40.

Lungo, Mario. 1994. "Redefining Democracy in El Salvador." In *Latin America Faces the Twenty-first Century*, edited by Susanne Jonas and Edward J. McCaughan, 142–59. Boulder, Colo.: Westview Press.

Malloy, James, and Mitchell Seligson, eds. 1987. *Authoritarians and Democrats: Regime Transition in Latin America*. Pittsburgh: University of Pittsburgh Press.

Marini, Ruy Mauro. 1980. "The Question of the State in the Latin American Class Struggle." *Contemporary Marxism* 1 (Spring): 1–9.

National Democratic Institute for International Affairs (NDI). 1991. *The 1990 National Elections in Guatemala: International Delegation Report*. Washington, D.C.: NDI.

Nun, José. 1991. "Democracy and Modernization, Thirty Years Later." Paper presented at the International Political Science Association meeting, Buenos Aires, July 21–26.

O'Donnell, Guillermo, Philippe Schmitter, and Laurence Whitehead, eds. 1986. *Transitions from Authoritarian Rule*. Baltimore: Johns Hopkins University Press.

Padilla, Luis Alberto. 1988. "Guatemala: Transición a la democracia?" *Estudios sociales centroamericanos* (San José) 47 (May–August): 37–49.

Peeler, John. 1992. "Elites and Democracy in Central America." Paper presented at the Seventeenth Congress of the Latin American Studies Association, Los Angeles, September 24–27.

Poitevín, René. 1991. *En busca de la identidad*. Cuaderno de FLACSO, no. 1. Guatemala City: FLACSO.

———. 1992. "Los problemas de la democracia." In *Los problemas de la democracia*, 11–45. Guatemala City: FLACSO.

Rosada Granados, Héctor. 1986a. "Guatemala, 1944–1985: Práctica política y conducta electoral." Guatemala City: ASIES. Manuscript.

———. 1986b. *Guatemala, 1985: Elecciones generales*. Guatemala City: ASIES no. 4.

———. 1989. "Transición política en Guatemala y sus perspectivas." *USAC: Revista de la Universidad de San Carlos* 6 (June): 57–65.

———. 1990. "Elecciones generales en Guatemala, 11 de noviembre de 1990 y 6 de enero de 1991." *USAC: Revista de la Universidad de San Carlos* (Guatemala) 11 (September): 73–85.

———. 1991. "El comportamiento de los partidos políticos en las elecciones 1990–1991." In *VII seminario sobre el rol de los partidos políticos en el proceso de elecciones, 1990–1991*, by Asociación de Investigación y Estudios Sociales (ASIES), 15–35. Guatemala City: ASIES.

Rosenberg, Tina. 1991. "Beyond Elections." *Foreign Policy* (Fall): 72–91.

Sarti, Carlos. 1987. "La democracia en Guatemala: Sus contradicciones, límites y perspectivas." *Cahiers* (December): 55–66.

Schmitter, Philippe, and Terry Karl. 1991. "What Democracy Is . . . and Is Not." *Journal of Democracy* (Summer): 75–88.

Solares, Jorge. 1992. "Guatemala: Etnicidad y democracia." In *Los problemas de la democracia*, 47–72. Guatemala City: FLACSO.

Solórzano, Mario. 1987. *Guatemala: Autoritarismo y democracia*. San José, Costa Rica: EDUCA/FLACSO.

2

ELECTIONS, CIVIL WAR, AND TRANSITION IN EL SALVADOR, 1982–1994: A PRELIMINARY EVALUATION

Enrique A. Baloyra-Herp

Could elections serve as efficacy tools of regime transition in a country without a culture of peaceful political contestation and citizen participation? Could this transition produce a democratic outcome in such a country in the middle of a civil war? The unreality of these propositions is what makes El Salvador's an extraordinarily interesting case of transition to democracy.

The Salvadoran elections of 1982–91 were criticized mainly on two grounds. One, they were orchestrated to convince the U.S. Congress and the international community that El Salvador was in a transition to democracy (Blachman and Sharpe 1988–89, 107; Herman and Brodhead 1984; Ulloa 1993, 21–22). Two, this pretense was thwarting the forging of elite compromise that permits democracy (Karl 1986, 10–12). By attributing major causal status to external conditions, critics overlooked factors and forces emerging anew in the region in the 1980s. But even critics knew that elections and the outcomes of transition often contradicted U.S. policy (Sharpe and Diskin 1984, 520–39; Karl 1985, 322–23; Karl 1986, 19; Blachman and Sharpe 1988–89, 109–19).

The election of 1982 probably drew the strongest criticism (Hadar and Studemeister 1982; Karl 1986, 13). However, it was not the United States but President José Napoleón Duarte and his closest advisers who, in October 1980, against the opposition of the Right and the early indifference of the Reagan administration, insisted on elections simply because nothing good was happening (Duarte 1986, chap. 5). This came before a July 16, 1981, speech by the assistant secretary of state for inter-American affairs, normally cited as proof that the elections were a North American initiative (Ceberio

and the absence of widespread fraud, violence, or intimidation; and (3) the right to organize as political parties and present candidates, giving voters a choice (Ozbudun 1987, 393). *Noncompetitive* elections "offer no options among candidates, voters lack freedom, and have no impact on the composition of a government created by a party monopoly." *Semicompetitive* elections are "a limited contestation among candidates who can stand for the assembly or parliament even though the mass media is monopolized by and the election outcome cannot alter the composition of the government" (Huneeus 1981, 108–9).

In the nineteenth century electoral outcomes were never final in El Salvador. Elections simply gauged popularity or ratified preelectoral agreements. In 1842 the defeat of Francisco Morazán and the collapse of the Central American Federation allowed Salvadorans to compete for the presidency in frequently held but rarely decisive elections. Elite pacts, violent overthrows of the executive, armed invasions, and constitutional conventions were utilized to install and legalize de facto governments. After 1860 presidential elections were less frequent and terms of office longer but more irregular (Arriaza-Meléndez 1989, 8–13; White 1973, 70–71). The overthrow of conservative president Francisco Dueñas, in 1871, opened a period of state consolidation, liberal rule, and expansion of the export economy (White 1973, 86–90).

Under the constitution of 1886, which lasted until 1939, presidential elections were held every four years, but incumbents not always finished their terms (Krennerich 1993, 307). In 1927 and in 1931, semicompetitive elections led to the presidencies of Pío Romero Bosque and of Arturo Araujo, who allowed more political participation and implemented mildly redistributive policies. In December 1931 Araujo was overthrown by his defense minister, General Maximiliano Hernández Martínez, who ruthlessly put down a peasant insurrection in the *matanza* of 1932 (Anderson 1971).

In the 1870s and 1880s, a very small group did not hesitate to use the power of the state in El Salvador to change land and labor legislation to its advantage (Lindo-Fuentes 1990, 131–51). Once consolidated as a landed oligarchy, this group became the most unforgiving opponent of democratization, both during the liberal oligarchic republic and beyond (Baloyra 1982, 22–32; Colindres 1977; Lindo-Fuentes 1990, 187–88; Menjívar 1980; Sebastián 1979; Sevilla 1984, 181–84; White 1973, 116–27). But, ever since the election of Araujo in 1931, Salvadoran politics have turned on the linkage between social equality and political participation. That diverse social groups might organize, introduce issues into the public agenda, and eventually turn them into policy was inimical to these landowners. After the collapse of the oligarchic republic in

Disorganization and High Turnout

Something must be clarified. The electoral system established in El Salvador during the 1980s was designed not to maximize popular participation but primarily to avoid fraud (CIDAI 1984, 214–18). This is a system based on distrust. In the early 1980s, Salvadorans established their voting eligibility by having a *cédula de identificación personal* (personal identity card—CIP) in their possession and their names appearing in the electoral registry. Article 5 of the Provisional Electoral Statute of 1982 (as amended) *presumed* that citizens presenting a valid CIP were included in the electoral registry and allowed them to vote "wherever they found themselves on election day regardless of their domicile" (CCE 1982b, 2–3). The Central Council of Elections (CCE) estimated about 2.5 million eligible voters. Segundo Montes provided a more accurate estimate of 2.25 million (Montes 1988, 180–81). What was then judged a disappointing turnout of "only" 1,551,687 voters in the constituent assembly election was in fact the *largest* of the entire period (see table 2.1).

In late 1983 and early 1984, a determined effort was made at purging and updating the electoral registry, but it fell short (CCE/CAO II 1984, 3–12; CIDAI 1984, 204–6). In the March 25, 1984, election, two precincts in each department had a copy of the *national* registry. This allowed anyone to vote there; otherwise voters had to find where to vote from CCE lists. Poll workers had a devil of a time helping illiterate citizens find their precincts (Kerstiens and Nelissen 1984a, 16–18; Meislin 1984a, 1984b). It was generally agreed that the elections were "very chaotic" (Chávez 1984; CIDAI 1984, 197; Meislin 1984c).[3] Salvadoran specialists suggested that registry flaws prevented some 275,000 people from voting and that another 87,811 could not vote because of procedural irregularities and logistical breakdowns (CIDAI 1984, 212–13). Foreign observers concluded that the effort to prevent fraud resulted in "a very complicated system which in the final instance [made] it very difficult for the electorate to actually vote" (Kerstiens and Nelissen 1984a, 16). Nonetheless, the March 1984 election posted the second-highest level of voting turnout in the *presidential* elections of 1982–94 (see table 2.1).

In April 1984 the conservative majority in the legislative assembly voted Decree No. 74, changing voting eligibility to be established by citizens presenting their CIPs without reference to the registry. Fearing that the conservatives had a treasure trove of CIPs, the Christian Democrats alleged that this invited large-scale fraud. President Alvaro Magaña vetoed the decree on grounds that the chaos of March 25 did not stem from an incomplete registry. Actually, there was no chaos in the presidential runoff of May 6 (Kerstiens and

Nelissen 1984b, 4). Voting turnout for the runoff was, and remains, second only to that of 1982.

To facilitate its protection by the armed forces, the CCE ran the March 1982 election with only 298 precincts (CUDI 1982, 582). This led to overcrowding, and voting became confusing (Anderson and Baloyra 1982). In addition, the CCE decided to mark the voters' thumbs with invisible instead of indelible ink. This complicated things. Some people could not vote in their municipalities because of war-related contingencies. Left parties denounced the election and asked their supporters to boycott it; the FMLN tried to sabotage the election (Baloyra 1982, 167–75). However, despite all these complications, more people voted in 1982 than at any other time.

Elections and Counterinsurgency

Voting turnout peaked during 1982–84, the period of worst violations of human rights, more sustained fighting in the war, and greater disorganization. But, beginning in the legislative elections of March 1985, there was a drastic decrease in voting turnout; about four hundred thousand voters were lost. Turnout would not regain the levels of the early 1980s until the end of the civil war (see table 2.1). During 1985–91 a high percentage of respondents in national surveys reported their intention to vote, but turnout did not exceed 60 percent—except in 1988. Why was this the case?

First, national and regional precincts were eliminated. The ARENA-dominated assembly reasoned that it was unfair for people from outside a town or municipality to vote for its legislative and local representatives (Asamblea Legislativa 1984). Although high turnout seemed to have favored his party in previous elections, President Duarte did not challenge the assembly on this. He vetoed two clauses of the bill, one forbidding the candidacies of close relatives of incumbents of national office (Art. 69.e) and another allowing parties running in coalition to have their logos printed separately on the ballot (Art. 94). The assembly overruled him. In May 1984 about 138,000 persons voted in regional precincts; most of them probably did not vote in March 1985. This requirement may have prevented close to 300,000 primarily displaced people from voting in subsequent legislative and municipal elections.

Second, beginning in 1985 there has been a steady decline of PDC voters. The presidency of Mr. Duarte was disappointing in many respects (Baloyra 1987; Sharpe 1986). He could not continue negotiations with the FMLN, begun at La Palma in October 1984, and could not turn the economy around (Karl 1985, 307–13). In 1986 the Democratic Popular Union (UPD), a coalition of peasant and labor organizations that had subscribed a "social pact" with Mr.

Table 2.2. *Nonindicative Participation in Recent Salvadoran Elections*

Year/Type	Votes Cast	Nonindicative Null	Nonindicative Blank	Votes Challenged	Nonindicative Total	Nonindicative %
1982 CA	1,485,185	131,498	51,438	6,412	182,936	12.3
1984 P	1,419,493	104,557	41,736	6,924	146,293	10.3
1984 RO	1,504,079	81,017	32,582	6,114	113,599	7.5
1985 L	1,101,606	74,007	57,690	4,678	131,697	12.0
1988 L	1,150,934	107,355	34,320	11,388	141,675	12.3
1988 M	986,086	100,390	38,270	11,076	138,659	14.1
1989 P	1,003,153	51,182	7,409	5,484	58,591	5.8
1991 L	1,153,013	59,998	34,508	7,026	101,532	8.8
1991 M	1,138,855	59,245	35,770	7,240	102,397	9.0
1994 P	1,411,320	70,503	28,311	4,849	103,663	7.3
1994 L	1,453,299	77,062	26,632	4,328	108,022	7.4
1994 M	1,449,249	73,752	27,225	4,003	104,980	7.2
1994 RO	1,246,220	40,048	5,461	3,467	48,976	3.9
1982–94	1,269,422	79,278	32,411	6,384	114,078	9.1

Sources: Annotated and computed from Consejo Central de Elecciones, *El Salvador, Elecciones Marzo 1982* (San Salvador: Consejo Central de elecciones, 1982), 164; CIDES Centroamérica, *El Salvador, Resumen 3* (March 28–April 3, 1984): 1; "Cómputos oficiales, 25 de marzo de 1984" and "Cómputos oficiales, 6 de mayo de 1984," *Estudios centroamericanos 39* (April–May 1984): 365–66; *Diario de Hoy*, April 2, 1984, 54; "Resultados provisionales," *Estudios centroamericanos 40* (April 1985): 223; "Resultados oficiales, 20 Marzo 1988," *Estudios centroamericanos 43* (March–April 1988): 285–95; Consejo Central de Elecciones, *Elecciones legislativas, 20 Marzo de 1988* (San Salvador: Consejo Central de Elecciones, 1988); Unidad de Planificación, *Información referente a los eventos electorales 1989–1991* (San Salvador: Tribunal Supremo Electoral, 1993); Tribunal Supremo Electoral, "Escrutinio Final," March 30, 1994 (presidential), April 5, 1994 (legislative), and April 7, 1994 (municipal); Tribunal Supremo Electoral, "Escrutinio Final," *Document 19*, April 27, 1994, 5:00 P.M.

Notes: Numbers for 1982–94 are averages of the single-year totals above. Abbreviations in the "Year/Type" column correspond to the following key:
- CA   Constituent Assembly
- L   Legislative
- M   Municipal
- P   Presidential
- RO   Presidential runoff

nal (PCN) and passed with the votes of PDC and PCN deputies, declared the suffrage "a right and duty of citizens whose exercise cannot be delegated nor renounced. Voting is *free*, direct, egalitarian, and secret" (cited by Montes 1988, 178).[4] This may have significantly deflated turnout.

Sixth, possession of the electoral *carnet* has a direct impact on voting turn-

Table 2.3. *Continued*

1994 (presidential), April 5, 1994 (legislative), and April 7, 1994 (municipal); Tribunal Supremo Electoral, "Escrutinio Final," *Document 19*, April 27, 1994, 5:00 P.M.

Notes: Numbers in parentheses are percentages. Percentage for 1982–94 is the average of the percentages of the vote. Their sums are larger than 100 percent. Numbers for 1982–94 are averages of the single-year totals above. Abbreviations in the "Year/Type" column correspond to the following key:

CA   Constituent Assembly
L   Legislative
M   Municipal
P   Presidential
RO   Presidential runoff

[a]Includes Democratic Action (Acción Democrática—AD), Salvadoran Popular Party (Partido Popular Salvadoreño—PPS), and Popular Orientation Party (Partido de Orientación Popular—POP).

[b]Includes AD, PPS, POP, Salvadoran Authentic Institutional Party (Partido Auténtico Institucional Salvadoreño—PAISA), and Stable Centrist Republican Movement (Movimiento Estable Republicano Centrista—MERECEN).

[c]Running as Nationalist Patriotic Union (Unión Patriótica Nacionalista—UPN) with the support of PAISA and PPS.

[d]Includes AD, Authentic Christian Movement (Movimiento Auténtico Cristiano— MAC), Popular Union (Unión Popular—UP), and Authentic Republican Party (Partido Auténtico Republicano— PAR).

[e]Includes AD, PAISA, POP, PAR, and Liberation (Liberación).

[f]Includes AD and MAC.

[g]Includes FMLN (287,811), Democratic Convergence (Convergencia Democrática— CD, 59,843), and National Revolutionary Movement (Movimiento Nacional Revolucionario—MNR, 9,431).

[h]Includes MAC, Unity Movement (Movimiento de Unidad—MU), and National Solidarity Movement (Movimiento de Solidaridad Nacional—MSN).

[i]Includes FMLN (276,124), CD (46,137), and MNR (6,546).

out. To register, voters present a *solicitud de inscripción en el Registro Electoral* (SIRE). If they do not have a CIP or birth certificate, they bring two witnesses to a local registration office *in their department of residence*. Then the CCE/TSE verifies the information. In one 1988 preelectoral survey about 11 percent of respondents anticipated not voting because they lacked the *carnet* (Martín-Baró 1988, 217); despite a deadline extension, the CCE managed to deliver *carnets* to only 84 percent of registered voters (Montes 1988, 181). Beginning in 1989, voters had to obtain their *carnets* at least thirty days in advance of the election. That year voting turnout was the second lowest. In March 1991 President Alfredo Cristiani initially opposed granting an extension. He later asked that voters who had completed their SIREs since August 1, 1990, and remained without their *carnets* be allowed to vote; seventy thousand may have benefited (Acevedo 1991, 509; OAS 1991, 229). Regardless, in 1991 there was an increase in valid votes probably because a left coalition presented candidates for the first time.

In July 1993 the Supreme Electoral Tribunal announced a massive registration drive. In October 1993, 28 percent of the public reported not having the *carnet* (IUDOP 1993, 1019). By November 19, a total of 786,386 citizens had

guerrillas. In addition, ARENA linked the PDC "communitarians" to crypto-Communists and State Department liberals, accused them of murdering several ARENA members, and asked the assembly to investigate the activities of U.S. ambassador Thomas Pickering. Salvadoran critics viewed the election and U.S. support for Mr. Duarte as part of the U.S. strategy in Central America (Ellacuría 1984, 301–4). It was generally agreed that the outcome was satisfactory to the United States (Ellacuría 1984, 303–4). On May 14, ARENA asked that the runoff be nullified on grounds of procedural irregularities. The challenge was disallowed. Duarte defeated D'Aubuisson by 752,625 to 651,741 votes. These totals are yet to be matched by anyone in El Salvador.

The elections of March 1985 were a watershed of sorts in that they closed a cycle of constructing democratic institutions and ending exceptionalism (Montes 1985, 215–16). Democratic leftists such as Mr. Ungo saw the elections "bring[ing] no changes in the power structure."[7] At a minimum, there were doubts that "procedurally flawed elections conducted under external pressure [had] largely failed to address most of the grievances that led to popular mobilization to begin with" (Booth 1989, 26). Presumably, elections could not firmly establish this connection in El Salvador until they were *fully* competitive.

In late 1987 Mr. Ungo's National Revolutionary Movement (MNR) and Rubén Zamora's Popular Social Christian Movement (MPSC) joined the recently created Social Democratic Party (PSD) in the Democratic Convergence (CD). A large plurality of the public regarded the return of these politicians as a positive development (IUDOP 1988a, 121). They explored the option of contesting the 1988 elections but were unable to raise money, field enough candidates and poll workers, and had little time to design and execute a coherent campaign. In 1989, running as the Democratic Convergence, they offered the candidacy of Mr. Ungo in the presidential race. The 1989 elections also marked a watershed in another respect: the FDR-FMLN alliance ceased to exist. Therefore, although more competitive, the elections did not include one active party to the armed conflict (Córdova Macías 1992, 40–41). Finally, ARENA consolidated its dominance as Alfredo Cristiani outdistanced PDC runner-up Fidel Chávez Mena by more than 150,000 votes.

Despite being the target of an isolated case of attempted fraud, the Convergencia did not challenge the validity of the elections of March 1991, which benefited from a slight increase in valid votes. The novelty of the Convergencia's running candidates for an enlarged legislative assembly (to eighty-four seats) and the election of twenty national deputies to the Central American Parliament may have offered additional incentives to voters.

Although there is room for debate about the competitiveness of previous elections, it is impossible to consider the Salvadoran general elections of 1994

local cadre throughout the country.[9] But the PDC cannot afford another split and subsequent rounds of soul-searching and recrimination. There is no telling where this would lead it. The "Fish" has done better as a reformist party. It needs to recover voters lost to ARENA but not by trying to outbid the Right as the efficient manager of a neoliberal agenda. It can recover some of its popular and peasant roots by not divorcing the populist-redistributionist Duarte legacy and by fielding better presidential candidates. Whichever the case, following the debacle of 1994, the PDC has much homework to do and quite an uphill climb to recovery.

For now the National Conciliation Party (Partido de Conciliación Nacional—PCN) remains the most relevant of the minor parties, the "one-half" option to complete the three-party party spectrum. The PCN was basically a machine party dependent on official favor. Like the PDC, the PCN is now at less than half the strength with which it entered the elections of the transition. The National Democratic Union (UDN), the old electoral front of the Communist Party of El Salvador (PCS), has practically disappeared from sight. Two minor parties, the Authentic Christian Movement (Movimiento Auténtico Cristiano—MAC), a splinter of the PDC, and Mr. Ungo's MNR, did not get the required minimum share of the 1994 legislative vote to renew their certification. Of the newcomers, only the Unity Movement (Movimiento de Unidad—MU) survived that test.

Conclusion

In 1982–85 Salvadoran elections were relatively free, fair, and competitive; despite many difficulties, they had decent levels of popular participation. In 1988–91 they were free, relatively fair, and competitive, but with lower levels of participation. There was no level playing field, except in terms of rules and procedures based on distrust that were designed to minimize the possibility of fraud and that required the contestants to remain vigilant.

Initially turnout appeared low, but the eligible population was smaller than estimated. Turnout was deflated by inevitable and contrived difficulties in registration and voting that made those elections more inaccessible to some participants, particularly the most humble citizens and the displaced. Turnout declined as people realized the limited efficacy of elections; in addition, they lost confidence in the political parties. Violence and intimidation prevented people from voting. Compulsory voting was ended in 1988.

Precisely because of these factors, one may conclude that although lower than in the rest of the isthmus, the levels of turnout in El Salvador are accept-

lesser level of voting. A tumult does not an election make; not everyone who shows up can actually vote. Some are discouraged easily, particularly illiterates. Repeated observation shows that illiterate voters are intimidated and occasionally overwhelmed by it all. They need to be given assistance the moment they enter a precinct and to be oriented to their designated *juntas receptoras del voto* (JRVs); anything else is an open invitation to desertion. Rendering this assistance could be assigned to nongovernmental organizations (NGOs), such as the Junta de Vigilancia, and to other groups representing society at large and eager to help. This would enable the Supreme Electoral Tribunal (Tribunal Supremo Electoral—TSE) to reduce the number of party workers at every precinct, particularly when their obvious role is to mill around the JRVs and display the party colors—another flagrant violation of the Electoral Code committed by everybody and denounced by no one.

Fourth, municipal elections should be brought in line with the scheme of proportional representation utilized in Legislative Assembly elections. The present system exaggerates the representation of the winner and is therefore undemocratic. This is important because local government is no longer trivial in El Salvador, and the recency of civil war suggests the wisdom of sharing power.

Finally, the future composition of the TSE is still unclear as of this writing. The ideal is a nonpartisan Electoral Tribunal. For the moment, a three-to-two or four-to-three balance between the more and less successful parties is all the system may afford. But enforcing impartial rules is vital in a country that still lags behind the rest of Central America in terms of political tolerance and system support (Seligson and Córdova Macías 1992). The point of departure could be the selection of a new TSE composed of party notables known for their sense of fairness and open-mindedness.

Unfortunately, the choice during the 1980s was not between elections and negotiations (Sharpe and Diskin 1984, 540–47). The same cultural perspectives and relative power balances that made elections difficult were the ones that caused the war in the first place. Therefore, whatever external interlocutors these elections might have had, their more relevant "demonstration effects" were those that reached the local elite and mass public. Fortunately, enough of them participated in these elections until the time was ripe for negotiation to become the endgame of the transition.

Notes

In memory of Ignacio Ellacuría, S.J., Ignacio Martín-Baró, S.J., and Segundo Montes, S.J. I am grateful to Tricia Juhn, Bruce Maivelett, S.J., Mauricio Osegueda, and Carlos Vergara

———. 1987. "The Seven Plagues of El Salvador." *Current History* 86, no. 524 (December): 413–16, 433–34.

Benítez-Manaut, Raúl. 1989. *La teoría militar y la guerra civil en El Salvador*. San Salvador: UCA Editores.

Blachman, Morris J., and Kenneth E. Sharpe. 1988–89. "Things Fall Apart in El Salvador: What's at Stake in the Presidential Election." *World Policy Journal* 6 (Winter): 107–39.

Booth, John A. 1989. "Elections and Democracy in Central America: A Framework for Analysis." In *Elections and Democracy in Central America*, edited by John A. Booth and Mitchell A. Seligson. Chapel Hill: University of North Carolina Press.

———. 1991. "National Revolts in Central America." *Latin American Research Review* 26, no. 1:33–73.

Cáceres-Prendes, Jorge. 1988. "Estado, sociedad y política en un contexto de insurgencia popular: El Salvador, 1980–1987." *Anuario de estudios centroamericanos* 14, no. 1–2:25–68.

Ceberio, Jesús. 1980. "La guerrilla salvadoreña rechaza la amnistía y el calendario electoral anunciado por la Junta." *El País*, October 17.

Centro de Cómputo y Centro de Información, Documentación y Apoyo a la Investigación (CIDAI). 1984. "Destapando la 'caja negra.' " *ECA* 39 (April–May): 197–218.

Centro Universitario de Documentación e Información (CUDI). 1982. "Las elecciones de 1982." *ECA* 37 (May–June): 573–96.

Chacón, Ricardo. 1984. "Las campañas de los partidos." *ECA* 39 (April–May): 229–50.

Chávez, Lydia. 1984. " 'Complete Disorder,' Poll-Watcher Says." *New York Times*, March 26.

Colindres, Eduardo. 1977. *Fundamentos económicos de la burguesía salvadoreña*. San Salvador: UCA Editores.

Consejo Central de Elecciones (CCE). 1982a. *El Salvador: Elecciones Marzo 1982*. San Salvador: Consejo Central de Elecciones.

———. 1982b. *Ley Electoral Transitoria*. San Salvador: Consejo Central de Elecciones.

———. 1984. *Ley Electoral Transitoria*. San Salvador: Consejo Central de Elecciones.

Consejo Central de Elecciones (CCE)/Comisión para la Atención de los Observadores (CAO II). 1984. "A Brief Explanation of El Salvador's Electoral Process," March 25. Mimeo. San Salvador.

Córdova Macías, Ricardo. 1992. "Procesos electorales y sistemas de partidos en El Salvador (1982–1989)." *Documentos de Trabajo*. Serie de Análisis de la Realidad Nacional. San Salvador: FundaUngo.

Departamento de Ciencias Jurídicas, Universidad Centroamericana. 1988. "Reflexiones jurídicas sobre el escrutinio final de las elecciones del 20 de Marzo." *ECA* 43 (May): 329–39.

Duarte, José Napoleón, with Diana Page. 1986. *Duarte: My Story*. New York: G. P. Putnam's Sons.

Eguizábal, Cristina. 1984. "El Salvador: Elecciones sin democracia." *Polémica*, nos. 14–15 (March–June).

Ellacuría, Ignacio. 1984. "Visión de conjunto de las elecciones de 1984." *ECA* 39 (April–May): 300–324.

Enders, Thomas O. 1981. "El Salvador: The Search for Peace." *Current Policy* 296, July 16.

Farah, Douglas. 1989. "El Salvador's Mayors Quit in Droves, Leftist Guerrillas Frighten Authorities." *Washington Post*, March 3.

Garber, Larry. 1988. "El papel de los observadores internacionales en elecciones recientes en Centroamérica." In *Elecciones y democracia en América Latina*, edited by Manuel Aragón-Reyes. San José, Costa Rica: Centro Interamericano de Asesoría y Promoción Electoral.

Gibb, Tom. 1992. "Elections and the Road to Peace." In *Is There a Transition to Democracy in El Salvador?*, edited by Joseph S. Tulchin with Gary Bland. Boulder, Colo.: Lynne Rienner.

Hadar, Arnon, and Marguerite Studemeister. 1982. "The March 1982 Election: A Deeper Look." *El Salvador Bulletin* 1, no. 7:1–2.

Herman, Edward S., and Frank Brodhead. 1984. *Demonstration Elections: U.S.-Staged Elections in the Dominican Republic, Vietnam, and El Salvador*. Boston: South End Press.

Huneeus, Carlos. 1981. "Elecciones no-competitivas en las dictaduras burocrático-autoritarias en América Latina, 1981." *Revista española de investigaciones sociológicas* 13 (January–March): 101–38.

Schwartz, Benjamin C. 1991. *American Counterinsurgency Doctrine and El Salvador*, R-4042-USDP. Santa Monica: Rand Corporation.

Sebastián, Luis de. 1979. "El camino económico hacia la democracia." *ECA* 35 (October–November): 947–60.

Seligson, Mitchell A., and Ricardo Córdova Macías. 1992. *Perspectivas para una democracia estable en El Salvador*. San Salvador: Instituto de Estudios Latinoamericanos.

Sevilla, Manuel. 1984. "Visión global de la concentración económica en El Salvador." *Boletín de ciencias económicas y sociales* 7 (May–June): 155–90.

Sharpe, Kenneth E. 1986. "El Salvador Revisited: Why Duarte Is in Trouble." *World Policy Journal* 3 (Summer): 473–94.

Sharpe, Kenneth E., and Martin Diskin. 1984. "Facing Facts in El Salvador." *World Policy Journal* 1 (Spring): 517–47.

Tribunal Supremo Electoral. 1993. "Código electoral 1993." *Diario oficial* 318, no. 16, January 25.

Ulloa, Felix, Jr. 1993. "Transición, democracia y procesos electorales en El Salvador." *Cuadernos del IEJES* (August): 7–48.

United Nations, Department of Public Information. 1992. *El Salvador Agreements: The Path to Peace.* DPI/1208-92614 (May).

United Nations, Observer Mission in El Salvador (ONUSAL). 1993. *Report.* Security Council. S/2606 (October 20).

———. 1994a. *Informe.* Consejo de Seguridad. S/1994/179 (February 16).

———. 1994b. *Report.* Security Council. S/1994/304 (March 16).

Weathers, Bynum E. 1990. "LIC Doctrine, Strategy, and Force Configuration in Guatemala and El Salvador." In *Responding to Low-Intensity Conflict Challenges*, by Stephen Blank, Lawrence E. Grinter, Karl P. Magyar, Lewis B. Ware, and Bynum Weathers, 127–76. Maxwell AFB, Ala.: Air University Press.

Webre, Stephen. 1979. *José Napoleón Duarte and the Christian Democratic Party in Salvadoran Politics, 1960–1972.* Baton Rouge: Louisiana State University Press.

White, Alastair. 1973. *El Salvador.* New York: Praeger.

tablishing and maintaining an enduring democratic order throughout much of the twentieth century. Since 1954 the country has had eleven heads of state, only five of whom were popularly elected.

The Liberal and National Parties date from the turn of the century. In the past, the two parties were separated by differing approaches to state involvement in the economy. Today, there are few differences in party ideology and platform. Together they command about 96 percent of the popular vote. Their support tends to be cross-class and spread evenly throughout the country, which is the size of the U.S. state of Tennessee.

Personalism and clientelism characterize Honduran politics. Both military and civilian groups have had difficulty adapting to democracy. Civilians have shown as much or greater resistance to responsible government as has the military. It was the military, not civilians, that took decisive reform efforts during the 1970s. These measures addressed agrarian structure through land reform, and they expanded and enhanced the role of the state in the country's economic management (Morris 1984).

However, throughout the 1980s, civilian rule was circumscribed because of the U.S.-sponsored counter-revolutionary efforts against the government of Nicaragua (Kinzer 1991). During much of this period, Honduras allowed its territory to be used as a staging ground for the anti-Sandinista military forces. National security issues took precedent over civil and human rights issues. Disappearances, politically related murders, and repression marked the political scene and diminished the quality of the country's emergent democracy (Americas Watch 1987). The Honduran armed forces embraced their national security mission with zest; elections were almost incidental to their powerful clasp of the country during this period.

Five elections have been held since 1980, as table 3.1 illustrates. The first gave the country a new constitutional assembly in 1980. A year later, the second election brought to the presidency a Liberal Party medical doctor, Roberto Suazo Córdova. Despite his best efforts to continue in office beyond his constitutional term, elections were again held in 1986 (Rosenberg 1989). One of the doctor's cabinet ministers, José Azcona Hoyo, was elected for the next four-year term, a period when the Central American Peace Accords reduced military-inspired hostilities in Nicaragua. Then again in 1989, voters went to the polls and brought to power the National Party, led by Rafael Leonardo Callejas. The Honduran-based Nicaraguan paramilitary force was dismantled in late 1990 and early 1991 and abandoned Honduras. After a decade of regional civil war, Honduras now could turn inward to the difficulties of its own sociopolitical system. Although Callejas provided the country with leadership in opening the economy, his mandate was ultimately

internal democratization (Liberal Party) in the 1980s, both parties have been able to maintain and expand their hold on the country's electorate.

Second, the country's two minority parties (PINU—Innovation and Unity Party; and the PDC—Christian Democratic Party) offered electoral opportunities for dissidents who chose to stay within the system, particularly during the early part of the 1980s. Table 3.1 illustrates the growing acceptance of the traditional parties during the 1980s. They have managed to gain wider acceptance during the decade—capturing 94 percent of the popular vote in the 1989 election compared with just 92 percent in the 1980 constitutional assembly elections. However, the most recent data suggest that nearly 35 percent of voters abstained from casting a ballot in the 1993 presidential elections compared with just 6 percent in the 1985 elections. What happened to voters in the latest election?

First, the campaign was one of the dirtiest in the country's recent electoral history. The National Party emphasized the alleged pro-Communist tendencies of the Liberal Party presidential candidate. The Liberal Party alleged the connections of the National Party candidate to death squad activity in the early 1980s. Second, both of the minor parties failed to capture those disaffected from the traditional parties. Finally, a punishment vote may account for the unexpectedly large margin of victory by the Liberal Party. It appears that voters were generally unhappy with the National Party's neoliberal economic program, which has favored the country's wealthier groups (Inforpress 1994).

Data from public opinion surveys support the general Honduran interest in elections. In a survey conducted by Bendixen and Law in 1985, 60 percent of Honduran voters indicated that they agreed "that the [1985] elections [were] evidence that the democratic process [was] now established" (Bendixen and Law 1986, 7).[1] As well, a 1992 opinion poll conducted by CID Gallup illustrates that a majority of Hondurans believed that elections can bring about change. The question was asked in the following way: "Some believe that things in Honduras will continue being the same regardless of who wins the elections. Others say that this is not the case, that things can change with elections. Others don't know. What is your opinion?" In response to this question, 55 percent of those polled stated that "things can change," whereas only 31 percent believed that "things will stay the same." The low percentage of those cynical about elections is suggestive of the interest in the country toward elections; as Booth's findings (Conclusion) suggest, Hondurans are active politically. Their activism should be understood, however, as a consequence of the country's pervasive patronage system, rather than as any indicator of the emergence of programmatic politics or agenda setting.

ing states (Pastor Fasquelle 1986). Although presidential elections were held throughout this period, debate about these issues was largely nonexistent.

Thus, for most of the 1980s, the Honduran military had a well-defined mission of national security. Its primacy in the country's political system was restored, and it acted as if the civilian-led government around it was a nuisance that could be endured and ignored.

With the global and regional environment transformed in the 1990s, the Honduran military now confronts the identity crisis that was postponed for more than a decade by regional hostilities. An October 1992 World Court ruling on the disputed border territories between Honduras and El Salvador allowed for both sides to declare victory, thereby defusing long-simmering hostilities that could have spilled over into renewed conflict between the two countries. The ruling undermines even more deeply the Honduran armed forces' claim that El Salvador constitutes a military security threat. It highlights the military's identity crisis even further.

At its core, the fundamental question centers on exactly what role, if any, the military has in Honduran society. There are other questions as well. Does the Honduran military really need an air force that must maintain advanced jet aircraft? Why is the police dependent on the military? What mechanisms are necessary for civilians to effect control over the military? Shouldn't the defense minister be a civilian who is responsive to the president rather than the military?

Some of these questions, raised in the late 1970s as the military was exiting from office, were largely left untouched during the 1980s. However, they have resurfaced with greater intensity and interest in the 1990s. They attack the heart of the system of prerogatives and privileges that the military has cultivated since the mid-1950s, when the professional armed forces were first constituted in the country.

Some accountability norms have evolved over time. There is a vague consensus that senior military officers should not overtly display political ambitions while on active duty. When General Edgardo Melgar-Castro intimated that he might be a candidate for civilian elections in the early 1980s, he was summarily deposed from his position as president of the country. General Gustavo Alvarez lost support within his senior military command when he became too closely associated with the country's business elite.

Senior officers are also expected to reject any and all civilian efforts to reduce, downsize, or strip the military of its budget and functions. General Walter López was ousted from his position as chief of the armed forces in 1985 when it was feared that he might make too many concessions to the newly elected Liberal Party government of José Azcona. General Arnulfo Cantarero

countries save Costa Rica, the armed forces and police are still not wholly subordinate to civilian authority."

The ambassador's insistent questioning of the military's role was rejected on a variety of grounds. In the first place, the U.S. policy maker's willingness to make public statements in Honduras about the military was generally repudiated by the military as intervention in the country's domestic affairs.

One case in particular illustrates the issue. Following the rape and disembowelment of a young female student in July 1991, the Honduran military refused to identify and arrest suspects in the case, largely because they were military officers themselves. However, it was the U.S. ambassador who publicly urged an investigation into the military's complicity, engendering a widespread national outcry for justice in the case. Students subsequently marched on the U.S. embassy to thank Arcos for his support.[2]

The Honduran military was uncomfortable with the ambassador's outspoken role because of his opinion-making influence in Honduran society and his willingness to cross the diplomatic line in calling attention to the country's difficulties. At one point in early 1992, the ambassador publicly stated that justice "should not be turned into a viper that only bites the barefoot . . . so those that wear boots are immune" (Farah 1993). Such was his impact that as the ambassador's tenure in Honduras neared its end, a caricature in one newspaper (La Tribuna, May 8, 1993) showed three large monkeys (military officers) mocking the ambassador's departure ("se va Arcos!"), implying that they would have the last laugh.

A second challenge has come from Honduras's civilian leadership. During the early part of the presidency of Rafael Leonardo Callejas, the Honduran Foreign Ministry took the leadership in crafting a regionwide Central American security treaty that called, in part, for the gradual reduction in the size of the region's armies. Although targeted initially at the larger forces in neighboring Nicaragua, El Salvador, and Guatemala, the measure had as an objective the gradual downsizing of the Honduran armed forces once the other militaries had taken similar measures.

The initiative died for lack of support. No regional leader except the president of Costa Rica would support it. Even President Callejas left his foreign affairs ministry exposed to the hostility of his armed forces—he was silent on the matter. He was subsequently criticized in the local media for his "duality" of views. Earlier he had talked about the necessity of regional disarmament.

However, he too publicly discarded the IMF-World Bank call for arms reductions, arguing that Honduran military expenditures barely exceeded 2 percent of the country's GDP. One media analysis rejected Callejas's figures,

for citizen security, the country's private sector had struck a major nerve in the military's system of control. Its police force had always been an institution of low prestige and morale. It had served as the army's dumping ground. According to one army officer, "to serve in the police as an official of the Armed Forces is to be purged and devalued professionally" (*La Prensa* 1978).

Although General Discua promised to study the proposal, no concrete action was taken. Indeed, according to one U.S. embassy official during that period, it appears that the country's police were weaker than ever. Military officials regularly raided their own police agents' school for qualified lower-level individuals to fill military specialty vacancies.

The general deterioration of public order in Honduras coupled with continuing human rights violations did lead to a significant concession from the military in early 1993. In the midst of growing accusations about military involvement in human rights violations and mounting pressure from popular organizations for action, President Callejas created an "ad hoc commission" to propose a restructuring of the country's police forces.

Given thirty days to develop recommendations to reform the country's security forces, the commission was chaired by Oscar Andrés Rodríguez, the archbishop of Tegucigalpa. Other participants included representatives from the four registered political parties, the Congress, Supreme Court, the military, and the media. Excluded from the group were some of the military's most persistent challengers, including human rights organizations that alleged direct military involvement in politically related assassinations and human rights abuses.

Callejas's March 1, 1993, announcement of the ad hoc commission was punctuated by a large military mobilization throughout the country's capital and other cities. Explained by the military as a necessary action in the face of reports of imminent terrorist activity by the Morazanista Patriotic Front (Frente Patriótico Morazanista—FPM), its street presence was a threatening message as well to civilian authority. It harkened back to the days when General Alvarez freely put troops in the streets to intimidate.[3]

Even before the ad hoc commission could render its findings, President Callejas took an important step by naming a three-person commission to manage the National Investigative Directorate (DNI). This measure, urged by the commission, was intended to help the police to redirect their efforts. But it was the first step in placing the investigative police under civilian control.

Indeed, weeks later, the ad hoc commission announced a set of historic measures. In a lengthy report presented on April 13, 1993, to President Callejas, the commission called for the creation of a prosecutor general's office and

Article 279. The Commander in Chief of the Armed Forces should be a general or senior officer with the rank of colonel or its equivalent, in active service, Honduran by birth and he will be elected by the National Congress from a list proposed by the Superior Council of the Armed Forces. . . .

In essence, it is the Congress that appoints the commander of the armed forces on the recommendation of the military itself. Then this commander has the constitutional right to mediate any orders to his troops that may be given by the president. The autonomy that the military has gained through the constitutional provisions results from concessions made to the military by the framers of the country's 1957 constitution. They essentially set the military up as a fourth branch of government, in addition to the executive, legislative, and judicial branches (Ropp 1984).

Moreover, the constitution further stipulates (Art. 281) that the head of the country's Joint Chiefs of Staff will replace the commander in chief of the armed forces in the event of his temporary absence. As Leticia Salomón points out (1992, 99), this stipulation is relatively new, having replaced an earlier article that allowed the minister of defense to substitute for the chief in the event of temporary absence. Salomón and others suggest that this measure is intended as further insulation from any political—that is, civilian—control of the military through the defense minister, who of course sits on the civilian cabinet.

Military Leadership

The instability of Honduran civil society is generally mirrored by the same instability within the Honduran armed forces. Since 1972 the armed forces have had nine commanders in chief, as table 3.3 illustrates.

Of the nine commanders in chief, only two have been appointed through constitutional means. The other seven have assumed the senior military command position through an irregular process largely determined by intrainstitutional forces and coalitions that have had little connection with nonmilitary interests.

The best illustration of the military's autonomy from external interests on matters of leadership can be found with the unexpected 1984 ouster of General Gustavo Alvarez Martínez. This hard-line military officer, the architect of Honduras's new national security role in the early 1980s and the intellectual author of the country's mini–dirty war during that period, was ignominiously stripped of power by his own troops in 1984 and sent into exile in Costa Rica.

selves and their tenuous cohesion based on a pattern of shifting coalitions and personalities. As the military searches for a new mission in the 1990s, the tendency toward internal instability is likely to sharpen.

The Military's Growing Financial Activity

Even as the Honduran armed forces are groping for a new military mission in the post–cold-war era, they have not lost sight of their material interests. Through a variety of instruments, the military has become a powerful economic force in the country. As pointed out by one journalist, "military-owned businesses can offer loans and credit cards, sell cement, broker real-estate deals, provide insurance, even embalm and bury the dead" (Johnson 1992).

The military's involvement in the economy is symptomatic of the absence of a strong, cohesive civilian presence in the country. Even though there has been a democratically elected government for more than a decade, the military still controls (see table 3.4) the telephone company, the major airports and seaports, immigration services, the merchant marine, and the national police. With the exception of the modest efforts concerning the police, there has been little, if any, concerted action to reduce military control of these important government agencies.

At the core of the military's economic domain is the Military Pensions Institute (IPM). Financed with funds appropriated by the government for military retirements, the IPM is an important player in the domestic economy. According to one report, the IPM's purpose is to build its portfolio so that each retired senior officer can have an annual income in excess of $100,000. Its major assets include the public access Armed Forces Bank (BANFAA), an insurance company (PREVISA), and a credit card company that makes cards available to the public (PREVICARD). The IPM has also competed in the market for companies being privatized.

Such serious involvement in the country's business affairs has prompted one observer to state that Honduran officers are "more like CEOs than soldiers" (Marquis 1991). In Honduras the military's economic presence is of great concern, especially among private-sector leaders who understand that the military's privileged political position can help it to translate into economic leverage. The IPM's recent efforts to purchase a state-owned cement company in the country were particularly troublesome to a number of Honduras's family-oriented investor groups. It is likely that the IPM will target other state-owned enterprises should they become available.

Defenders of the military argue that its pension system is smaller than the teachers' and state employees' funds and that the only way to provide for the

the impunity of the armed forces and police to the rule of law. This impunity is most apparent in the field of human rights, in which violations persist and for the most part go unpunished. According to one report (U.S. Embassy 1992) on human rights in Honduras, members of the country's armed forces enjoy this impunity for a number of reasons: (1) the country's Supreme Court has avoided making the difficult decision about the jurisdiction of civilian courts over armed forces personnel accused of offenses involving civilians; (2) civilians have little ability to levy formal accusations before military courts; (3) the country's court system has minimal credibility, little capacity, and no sustained history of successfully judging the military; (4) even if the court system had some capacity to address military violations, the armed forces tend to protect those personnel, especially officers, accused of abuses.

There are notable exceptions. A Honduran judge's decision in mid-1993 to give relatively lengthy sentences (by Honduran standards) to two military officials accused in the July 1991 rape and disembowelment of the student mentioned above has been viewed by many in Honduras as a triumph for civilians over the military (INCEP 1993). However, for this highly publicized case to be completed, it took the intervention of the U.S. ambassador, open mobilization by the public against the armed forces, and the intense interest of the international human rights community.

The military is not alone in enjoying immunity from the legal system. As the U.S. Embassy's report states, "the same immunity from prosecution and punishment enjoyed by military personnel is extended to other elite groups. Virtually no elected official, member of the business elite, bureaucrat, politician, or anyone with perceived influence or connection to the elite was subjected to legal sanctions for serious abuses" (U.S. Embassy 1992, 1–2).

Conclusion

What happens if a transition to democracy takes place and yet the very beneficiaries of the transition are ill prepared to take advantage of it? This is exactly the case in Honduras. Although the electoral mechanisms to promote democracy are now firmly in place, and although the country's political elite now seems to accept these mechanisms, it is clear that they are less comfortable with other aspects of consolidating democracy.

Why should the country's political elite be reticent about taking the steps necessary to reduce the military's autonomy and impunity? First, as has been illustrated, there is a forty-year tradition of military autonomy in the country.

References

Americas Watch. 1987. *Human Rights in Honduras: Central America's Sideshow.* New York: Human Rights Watch.

Arcos, Crescencio. 1991. "Managing Change in Central America." *Foreign Service Journal* 68, no. 4 (April).

Bendixen, Sergio, and John Law. 1986. *The Political Pulse of Latin America: Voter Attitudes in El Salvador, Colombia, Guatemala, Peru, and Honduras.* New York: SIN Television Network.

Caribbean and Central America Report. 1993. April 1.

Farah, Douglas. 1993. "Honduras Assesses Role of Its Military." *Washington Post,* April 24.

Hammond, Tony. 1991. "The Role of the Honduran Armed Forces in the Transition to Democracy." Master's thesis, University of Florida.

Inforpress. 1994. "Honduras: Reina cumple sus primeros cien días." *Inforpress centroamericana,* May 19.

Instituto Centroamericano de Estudios Políticos (INCEP). 1993. "Honduras: Avance de la administración de justicia tras condena a militar." *Panorama centroamericano/Reporte político* 84 (July).

Johnson, Tim. 1992. "Honduran Military's Second Mission, Profit." *Miami Herald,* March 10.

Kinzer, Stephen. 1991. *Blood of Brothers: Life and War in Nicaragua.* New York: G. P. Putnam's Sons.

La Prensa. 1978. September 15.

Latin American Weekly Report. 1992. October 15.

La Tribuna. 1991. October 4.

Marquis, Christopher. 1991. "After Huge Buildup, U.S. Seeks a Leaner Honduran Military." *Miami Herald,* August 16.

Meza, Victor. 1990. "Elecciones en Honduras: Un intento de interpretación." *Honduras, Especial* 48 (July).

Molina Chocano, Guillermo. 1992. "Elecciones y consolidación democrática en Honduras en la última decada." In *Una tarea inconclusa: Elecciones y democracia en América Latina.* San José, Costa Rica: IIDH/CAPEL.

Morris, James A. 1984. *Honduras: Caudillo Politics and Military Rulers.* Boulder, Colo.: Westview Press.

Oseguera de Ochoa, Margarita. 1987. *Honduras hoy: Sociedad y crisis política.* Tegucigalpa: CEDOH.

Pastor Fasquelle, Rodolfo. 1986. "Derechos humanos en Honduras: Una situación distinta.: In *Honduras: Realidad nacional y crisis regional,* 133–38. Tegucigalpa: Centro de Documentación de Honduras.

Ropp, Steve. 1984. "National Security." In *Honduras: A Country Study.* Washington, D.C.: Government Printing Office.

Rosenberg, Mark B. 1989. "Can Democracy Survive the Democrats?: From Transition to Consolidation in Honduras." In *Elections and Democracy in Central America,* edited by John A. Booth and Mitchell A. Seligson, 40–59. Chapel Hill: University of North Carolina Press.

Salomón, Leticia. 1992. *Política y militares en Honduras.* Tegucigalpa: Centro de Documentación de Honduras.

Tiempo. 1991a. September 20.

———. 1991b. October 19.

U.S. Embassy. 1992. *Human Rights Report.* Tegucigalpa.

meaningful political participation. Peasants were sometimes forced to serve in one or the other of the contending armies in a battle for control of the state. Alternatively, they were sometimes lured to "vote" in fraudulent elections with bribes of food and drink. Military competition for state control made survival quite difficult among Nicaragua's peasantry. Many villages and individuals preferred to stay out of politics altogether and hopefully, thereby, to stay alive. One common story recounts that Nicaraguan villages kept one portrait each of the ruling generals of the Liberal and Conservative armies. When one army thundered through the village, peasants would hurriedly hang up the portrait of the appropriate general, only to change the portrait when the opposing army arrived. The story illustrates a phenomenon that to some extent persists today—a chameleonlike quality of outwardly expressed "public opinion" among parts of Nicaragua's populace. Each village seemed primarily concerned with presenting the "public opinion" that the army wanted to hear. The Nicaraguan tendency to disguise public opinion around the issue of who should rule grew so entrenched that some observers argue that it became a national tradition with a name—the *güegüense* tradition.

In the late 1920s this pattern was broken when some of Nicaragua's peasantry expressed genuine and unsolicited political opinion by rallying behind nationalist revolutionary Augusto Sandino. Sandino was not from among Nicaragua's elite and had spent time as a worker in Mexico. Impressed by the Mexican Revolution, he returned to Nicaragua in 1927 concerned about the poverty of the population as well as the extent of U.S. influence in the country. Although Sandino initially took up arms as part of one of the two elite-controlled armies engaged in the long-standing struggle for political control, he soon developed his own agenda. This included driving the U.S. Marines out of Nicaragua and redistributing land to landless peasants (Walker 1986; Macaulay 1985). Both causes apparently struck sympathetic notes among Nicaragua's poor majority. Sandino's "Crazy Little Army" of peasants and the poor withstood U.S. Marines and Nicaraguan National Guard counterinsurgency warfare for six years until the United States withdrew its forces in 1933. Sandino also established agrarian cooperatives for his followers in a region that his army controlled. The strength and extent of Sandino's following were an early expression of autonomous popular political opinion and participation in a country where these were rarely repressed. The vehemence of the popular expression frightened elites, and Sandino was assassinated in 1934. However, his political program and the popular following it amassed were portents of popular politics in later decades.

The Sandino affair was followed by the Somoza years during which one family (a father, followed by his two sons) ruled the country as despots from

course, had very limited and unsuccessful experience with expressing itself through elections. Before 1979 Somoza had often frustrated the opposition through repression or fraud. Moreover, several of the parties who opposed the FSLN in 1984 had themselves sometimes been involved with Somoza in engineering electoral fraud during the years of the dictatorship. Thus the opposition parties in 1984 had almost no experience with bidding for popular support in a legal fashion or with expressing their opposition to the incumbent through electoral channels.

The lack of experience with fair elections and the lingering revolutionary popularity of the Sandinistas made Nicaragua's first election in 1984 highly unusual. First, the incumbent Sandinistas enjoyed a major advantage in the form of revolutionary success and charisma. Second, the opposition parties seemed to spend as much energy disagreeing with one another as they did opposing the Sandinistas.[5] As a result the Sandinista party faced no fewer than six opposition parties, including remnants of the traditional Liberal and Conservative Parties. Despite the newness of the experiment, however, the Nicaraguan population seems to have embraced the election—91 percent of the registered population voted (LASA 1984, 17). Given the revolutionary popularity of the FSLN, the still recent memory of FSLN courage in the revolutionary struggle, and the splintered nature of the opposition, it is not surprising that the Sandinistas won the 1984 election by a landslide, taking 67 percent of the vote. The second strongest party, the Conservatives, took 14 percent. The Liberals won 9 percent of the electorate (LASA 1984, 17).

Although 1984 marked Nicaragua's first authentic election and popular support for the Sandinistas was clear, the election received very little positive attention in the United States. Coming at the height of the Reagan years, the election was dismissed both by the administration and by the media. Both argued that the Sandinistas had coerced the results and that the election had not been fair (Robinson 1992).

Nicaragua's 1990 Election

Nicaragua held its second election in February 1990. That election was markedly different from 1984, both in the way it was handled internally and in the international attention it received. Everyone seemed to be learning about conducting elections in Nicaragua. The Sandinistas again ran as the incumbent party. The opposition, however, changed its tactics entirely. Realizing that no opposition party alone could defeat the Sandinistas, most of the opposition parties banded together in one umbrella coalition: the United Nic-

tioned. Entire families lost jobs. Workers often could not make ends meet even when they retained their salaries. Finally, pressure on Nicaragua from international financial institutions forced the government to roll back many reforms it had put in place during the first five years of the revolution. As a result Nicaraguans lost many of the social benefits they had come to see as major gains of the revolution and on which they had come to depend as the economic situation worsened.

In addition to the disastrous economic situation, the war against the U.S.-financed anti-Sandinista rebels (the contras) slowly wore out the Nicaraguan people. When the war had begun in the early 1980s, many Nicaraguans had enthusiastically supported the Sandinista effort to stop the contras, many of whom were seen by Nicaraguans as former members of Somoza's National Guard.[6] In addition, the contras habitually attacked unarmed civilians and civil servants such as teachers, doctors, nurses, and agricultural technicians as well as schools, factories, and medical clinics. Initially it was not difficult to rouse popular opposition to the contras. Over the years, however, the resolve of the Nicaraguan people understandably weakened. The war dragged on and on with more young men killed each week. The conflict was a huge economic drain on a broken economy. Each soldier was a dependent to be fed and clothed rather than a productive citizen. Individual families could not afford to lose a breadwinner even temporarily to the army, much less permanently to death. Eventually the economic crisis and the growing unpopularity of government policies made some sectors increasingly receptive to the contras' position, particularly in the rural north and east and among the informal sector in Managua. Sickened by war and exhausted by the economic crisis, Nicaraguans were desperate for peace and prosperity. They wanted goods available in the stores and their loved ones home from the front. Anxious to be out from under U.S. pressure, both economically and militarily, Nicaraguans took their exhaustion and anxiety with them to the polls in 1990.

As in 1984, the Nicaraguan population again embraced the election, this time with a voting rate of 86 percent of the registered population. In the election Violeta Chamorro defeated the Sandinista candidate by 54.7 percent to 40.8 percent. After a series of negotiations of details of the transition and a cease-fire with the contras, Ortega quietly ceded power to the new president. Although UNO actually carried only slightly more than half of the vote, when compared with the Sandinista percentage UNO's margin of victory was a virtual landslide. The magnitude of the Sandinista defeat is even greater when compared with the 67 percent it had received just six years earlier. Moreover, for the most part, both within Nicaragua and in the United States, the Sandinista defeat was unexpected, a surprise and even a shock for supporters of both

remainder of this essay I will assess the implications of the 1990 election for the Nicaraguan democracy, including the role played by the preelectoral surveys.

The earliest surveys of Nicaraguan public opinion prior to the 1990 election were conducted seven months before the election in August 1989.[11] This was an unusual and interesting time to be examining preelectoral public opinion. In August 1989 UNO did not yet formally exist. While it was clear that many parties opposed the Sandinistas, as they had in 1984, it was far from clear that these opposition parties would be able to swallow their differences enough to coalesce under an opposition umbrella. Thus, when these early surveys were done, the Sandinistas looked like the only cohesive and viable major party capable of entering the election campaign. In an early survey by the Nicaraguan research institute Itztani, among respondents who gave any partisan opinion at all, the Sandinistas had a definitive lead over all the opposition parties combined. The survey showed 32 percent supporting the Sandinistas and only 19 percent supporting all the opposition parties combined. These general contours of public opinion continued throughout the fall of 1989 and were responsible for initiating the generalized impression, both in the United States and in Nicaragua, that the Sandinistas were far ahead in public preference.

Yet omens of trouble for the FSLN also appeared in these early surveys and were generally ignored. Many and sometimes even most respondents in these early surveys did not give a partisan opinion at all. They refused to answer questions about candidate preference or avoided such questions by evasive tactics. The Nicaraguan *güegüense* tradition seemed to be reappearing, unnoticed by electoral observers. The general approach to evaluating public opinion polls is to treat nonrespondents (persons who refuse to answer) as "undecideds" and to omit them from the analysis. Analysts consider that the nonrespondent/undecideds will eventually decide whom they prefer and divide their vote largely along the same lines as did those who gave a partisan response. Thus partisan respondents are considered to "represent" nonrespondents, so that the latter may safely be ignored. This general approach led many opinion pollsters to predict the election based only on respondents who had given an opinion and thus to call a Sandinista lead.

In retrospect, however, this practice, while possibly defensible in established democracies, was highly questionable in Nicaragua.[12] First, the number of nonrespondents on the expected vote questions was high. While nonresponse rates of 10–15 percent are considered normal in advanced democracies, these early surveys drew nonresponse rates of 30–50 percent! Why did so many decline to name their presidential choice? In the politicized atmosphere of revolutionary Nicaragua, were that many people really undecided?

Figure 4.1. *Nicaraguan Elections: Survey Results, Prediction, and Actual Vote*

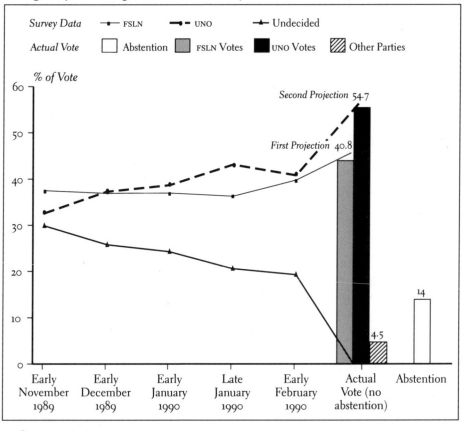

Source: DOXA surveys.

Note: See text for methodology of projection; abstention excluded in projection.

ever, like many other polling organizations, DOXA also received a high non-response rate on the expected vote question. Also like other organizations, DOXA did not consider the nonrespondents when predicting electoral results. If these nonrespondents are actually counted as UNO voters, the electoral predictions that emerge come even closer to the actual electoral results than do even DOXA's actual predictions.

Figure 4.1 indicates the trends of survey results that DOXA obtained during the months preceding the election. These data draw on a question in which respondents were asked who they thought would win the election. In the graph nonresponse rates decline substantially between the first survey and the last. In addition, both FSLN support rates and UNO support rates rise, with UNO support staying steadily ahead of FSLN support. On the basis of these results

dents voted in the election for the person they said they supported at the point of DOXA's last survey. Third, let us assume that all of DOXA's respondents voted in the election itself. (This is a far-fetched one, since we know that 14 percent of the eligible electorate did not vote.) Finally, let us assume that DOXA's respondents did not change their minds between UNO and the FSLN—they made a partisan choice and stuck with it. If they shifted, it was only from a nonrespondent to a partisan supporter. If one accepts these assumptions, we find that, based on DOXA's data, one can predict the electoral outcome even more closely than we have already done in figure 4.1.

If we compare slope rates among the three lines in figure 4.1, we can see that both FSLN support and UNO support increase during the study but at different rates. Support for the FSLN increases only slightly for an upward slope of .46; UNO support increases a good deal more, for a total upward slope of 1.64. As these slopes increase, the number of nonrespondents or the non-response slope actually decreases, by 2.12 (slope $= -2.12$). How much of the 2.12 total downward slope among the nonrespondents went to UNO and how much went to the FSLN?

We can learn this by dividing each of the positive slopes (.46 for the FSLN and 1.64 for UNO) by the downward slope of the nonrespondents (2.12). If we do this (and assume that all nonrespondents voted), then we see that 77.36 of nonrespondents may have supported UNO in the final election and only 22.64 percent went for the FSLN. In the final DOXA survey 19.3 percent were nonrespondents. If we take 77.36 percent of those and assign them to UNO and take 22.64 percent and assign them to the FSLN, we come surprisingly close to the actual electoral results. These additions predict a UNO vote of 55.73 percent and an FSLN vote of 44.17 percent. The estimate slightly overestimates support for both parties (because it underestimates voter abstention). In the actual election UNO took 54.7 percent and the FSLN 40.8 percent. Calculations based on these assumptions allow an electoral prediction that comes closer than DOXA's own predictions, which were themselves made without using the nonrespondents. It also comes closer to the actual electoral outcome than our own more conservative prediction in figure 4.1.

Of course, in actually forecasting an election one cannot make as many assumptions as we have made here. In retrospect DOXA was correct in forecasting more conservatively and in *not* including the nonrespondents in any official prediction. It is also important to remember that these results are *aggregate* results, lumping together and comparing opinion trends across all respondents to all surveys. This is not to say that 77.36 percent of nonrespondents voted for UNO. Some may have voted for the FSLN while the latter lost some of its supporters to UNO. However, the surprising closeness we achieve to

which democratic rules have become a part of political reality for the average person. Indeed, the success or failure of survey research may be a more accurate reflection of the health of Nicaraguan democracy than is the formal institution of national elections.

Nicaraguans may hold and vote in national elections. They may place civilian regimes in power. If this practice continues over a long period of time, then Nicaragua may be said to enjoy a formal, constitutional democracy. If, however, members of the public sampled at random by survey researchers do not feel comfortable expressing their opinions and do not trust that their opinions will remain confidential, then Nicaraguan democracy is more shallow than these institutional aspects imply. If such secretiveness and camouflage of opinions remain common in election after election, then the health and progress of democracy in Nicaragua will have been seriously constrained. It will suggest that elections are not being conducted in a free and open atmosphere. In the long run, such conditions will not be conducive to the stabilization of formal democracy in Nicaragua because regimes may be unstable, unpopular, and elected only as the result of pressure. In such circumstances elections will be only formal and superficial and will not have contributed to a popular culture of openness, dialogue, and participation under democratic rules.

What were Nicaraguans afraid of? Partisans of each color blame the other side. Supporters of UNO say that the Sandinista regime was repressive and always pressured the public. The Sandinistas, in contrast, argue that U.S. pressure influenced the election in far more fundamental but indirect ways. Sandinista supporters say Nicaraguans were afraid to vote for the FSLN because they dreaded a continuation of the economic blockade, other economic pressure, and the contra war. It is likely that both sides are correct. It is possible that Nicaraguans felt unjustly pressured by both sides and from many different directions. It is also possible that these fears were exaggerated or even unjustified. Perhaps many Nicaraguans felt pressured and fearful because they were used to feeling repressed and fearful—a sort of political cultural vicious circle. Yet regardless of the source of the reluctance to answer or of whether and how far feelings of fear were justified, clearly the perception of pressure or risk was there for some of the electorate.

All of this would seem to indicate that the 1990 Nicaraguan election was a good deal less democratic than its formal appearance would lead us to believe. Whether or not the public actually was pressured is secondary to the fact that the public *felt* pressured. True or not, justified or not, that perception reflects something of the nature of democracy in Nicaragua. Just how far the undemocratic atmosphere went in affecting the final vote is impossible to know. Would a less pressurized atmosphere have resulted in different percentages

election, then the depth and quality of political participation are limited among those who feel fearful and who do not respond. When elections occur in a pressurized atmosphere, including heavy-handed U.S. involvement, then they have lacked an environment conducive to the exercise of full, participatory rights by everyone. If a president has been elected in an atmosphere in which citizens have felt pressured to vote in one way or another, then the election may not have helped consolidate a stable regime at all. If elections have created an excuse for domestic or foreign actors to pressure or intimidate the population, then elections have not contributed to a participatory political culture. And finally, if the United States or other foreign power has had a negative, dominant role in domestic economics and politics for years before the election, then Nicaraguan freedom to exercise democratic rights has been seriously compromised.

The survey results surrounding the 1990 election indicate that all of the above nondemocratic influences were or may have been present in 1990. Elections in Nicaragua, and particularly in 1990, therefore offer a mixed indicator about the development of democracy in Nicaragua. The elections themselves are a step in a democratic direction. The atmosphere and pressure (real and perceived) surrounding the 1990 election make that step a good deal smaller than it otherwise might have been. This mixed assessment of democracy in Nicaragua in the past leaves us with uncertainty about democracy in Nicaragua in the future. Nicaragua has continued under Chamorro's civilian regime for five years now. Although there have been threats to Chamorro's presidency, she has fended them off successfully so far. The future health and stability of democracy in Nicaragua will improve only if minimal conditions are met: Nicaragua will need repeated elections at regular intervals. The next should be held on schedule in 1996. The national and international context will need to allow the FSLN to compete and win, as well as to take and hold office. If it regains office, the FSLN will need to pay more careful attention to democratic rules than it did in the past. Democracy in Nicaragua has taken a small step in the right direction against overwhelming odds. Whether or not that progress continues is uncertain and bears careful watching.

Notes

I would like to thank John Booth and Mitchell Seligson for helpful comments on an earlier draft of the present chapter.

1. Although these were Nicaragua's freest elections in a relative and historical sense, they were still subjected to heavy external pressure and manipulation (LASA 1984, 1990).

leaves out the first survey, since it asked different questions. With each survey DOXA interviewed between eight hundred and twelve hundred people.

15. For further discussion of this issue, see the controversy in the *American Journal of Political Science* among Bischoping and Schuman (1992, 1994), Anderson (1994a), and Booth (1994).

16. Although I suspect that nonresponse was the key to forecast failures, other scholars have also investigated the problem and derived different answers. Schuman (1990) and Bischoping and Schuman (1992) maintain that interview bias, both real and perceived, was responsible for incorrect poll results. Their findings infer a need for deliberate bias in future research policy in order to achieve correct results. Other authors who have considered the issue include Barnes (1992), Robinson (1992), and Oquist (1992).

References

Anderson, Leslie. 1992. "Surprises and Secrets: Lessons from the 1990 Nicaraguan Election." *Studies in Comparative International Development* 27:3.

——. 1994a. "Neutrality and Bias in the 1990 Nicaraguan Preelection Polls: A Comment on Bischoping and Schuman." *American Journal of Political Science* 38:486–94.

——. 1994b. *The Political Ecology of the Modern Peasant: Calculation and Community*. Baltimore: Johns Hopkins University Press.

——. N.d. "Uncharted Waters: Electoral Democracy in Post-Socialist Societies: The Case of Nicaragua." Manuscript in progress.

Barnes, William. 1992. "Rereading the Nicaraguan Pre-Election Polls in the Light of the Election Results." In *The 1990 Elections in Nicaragua and Their Aftermath*, edited by Gary Provost and Vanessa Castro, 41–128. Lanham, Md.: Rowman and Littlefield.

Barry, Tom. 1987. *Roots of Rebellion: Land and Hunger in Central America*. Boston: South End Press.

Bischoping, Katherine, and Howard Schuman. 1992. "Pens and Polls in Nicaragua: An Analysis of the 1990 Preelection Surveys." *American Journal of Political Science* 36:331–50.

——. 1994. "Pens, Polls, and Theories: The 1990 Election Revisited." *American Journal of Political Science* 38:495–99.

Bollinger, William. 1992. "Public Opinion and Democracy in El Salvador and Nicaragua." Paper presented at the Seventeenth International Congress of the Latin American Studies Association, Los Angeles, September.

Booth, John A. 1985. *The End and the Beginning: The Nicaraguan Revolution*. 2d ed. Boulder, Colo.: Westview Press.

——. 1994. "Assessing Candidate Preference Polling and Other Survey Research in Nicaragua, 1989–1990: Comments on Anderson, and Bischoping and Schuman." *American Journal of Political Science* 38:500–513.

Finkel, Steven E., Thomas M. Guterbock, and Marian Borg. 1991. "Race of Interviewer Effects in a Pre-election Poll." *Public Opinion Quarterly* 55, no. 3:313–30.

Gould, Jeffrey. 1990. *To Lead as Equals: Rural Protest and Political Consciousness in Chinandega, Nicaragua, 1912–1979*. Chapel Hill: University of North Carolina Press.

Gunther, Albert C. 1992. "Biased Press or Biased Public? Attitudes toward Media Coverage of Social Groups." *Public Opinion Quarterly* 56, no. 2:147–67.

Latin American Studies Association (LASA). 1984. "The Electoral Process in Nicaragua: Domestic and International Influences." Report of the Latin American Studies Association Delegation to Observe the Nicaraguan Election. Austin, Tex., November 19.

——. 1990. "Electoral Democracy under International Pressure." Report of the Latin American Studies Association Commission to Observe the 1990 Nicaraguan Election. Pittsburgh, March 15.

Lund, Daniel. 1990. "Polling Failure in Nicaragua Assessed." *Interamerican Public Opinion Report* (Spring): 1–5.

5

ELECTIONS AND DEMOCRACY IN COSTA RICA

Cynthia H. Chalker

The tiny and rather poor Central American republic of Costa Rica seems an unlikely site for democracy. Statistically, both low levels of economic development and small size are associated with authoritarian government.[1] Yet Costa Rica has the longest tradition of stable democratic rule in Latin America, a region where only a handful of countries have enjoyed extended periods of democracy. Citizens enjoy protection of their civil and political rights, and elections are honest and free.[2] In the context of Central America, Costa Rica appears even more exceptional. With a history of civil war, repressive military rule, and foreign intervention, other states in Central America have experienced remarkably high levels of violence and repression.

Most explanations of why Costa Rica is democratic rely on geographic and economic factors to account for the emergence and stability of democracy.[3] Perhaps the most common explanation credits the country's poverty and geographic isolation, beginning in the colonial period. Without mineral wealth or an indigenous population to exploit, Costa Ricans of all classes turned to tilling the land and so created an egalitarian society. Attempts to explain democracy rely heavily on this image, often making democracy appear as an inevitable outcome of the social and economic structure of the country. However, recent research challenges this picture of Costa Rican development. For example, Gudmundson (1986, 1) argues that the image of Costa Rica as an isolated, egalitarian agrarian society is "one of the most attractive and widely disseminated national mythologies of any Latin American nation." Yet this account of early rural life in Costa Rica can be found in numerous historical accounts and continues to inform contemporary political dialogue (see Gudmundson 1986).

have slowly lost control over finance, planning, provision of services, and administration of development projects (Vega 1992).[6]

The president is directly elected for a four-year term and cannot be re-elected.[7] The executive formally shares power with his cabinet ministers. In administration of the bureaucracy, budget writing, legislative initiative, and the exercise of veto and decree powers, the approval of the relevant cabinet minister is required. However, since the president alone appoints and removes members of his cabinet, the effective constraint on executive power is minimal. In policy making, the executive branch tends to dominate the legislative agenda, despite the independence and strength of the other branches.[8]

The constitution gives most formal powers to the unicameral, fifty-seven-member Asamblea Nacional (National Assembly). Deputies serve four-year terms, concurrent with that of the executive, and cannot be elected to consecutive terms. The assembly has the power to legislate, tax, declare war, impeach and censure government officials, approve the national budget, demand information from government ministers, and appoint justices of the Supreme Court and the Constitutional Court (Sala IV) and may override a presidential veto by a two-thirds vote. Equally important are the assembly's oversight of the executive and its function as a national forum for debate (Gutiérrez 1992). The assembly is also a site of heavy lobbying efforts by organized groups.

One of the most remarkable provisions in the 1949 constitution is the abolition of the armed forces and a prohibition against creating a standing army. Despite these provisions, it is not the case that Costa Rica has no armed forces. The Civil Guard, Rural Guard, and the Organization for National Emergencies do make up a national militia. The threat of an armed takeover of the government is effectively eliminated because the forces are not professionalized. Despite training and funds from the United States in the 1980s, the forces remain poorly trained and lightly armed and have a turnover rate between governments as high as 50 to 90 percent (Ameringer 1982b, 47). The high turnover occurs because the guards are the principal source of patronage positions and are typically staffed by appointees loyal to the party in power.

The Catholic Church in Costa Rica has most often supported socially progressive movements but has only a weak presence in politics. The church does play an important role in legitimating political power. For example, one of the first acts of a newly elected president is to meet with the archbishop and ask his blessing for the new administration. Ameringer (1982b, 73) argues that the extensive social welfare provisions of the Costa Rican government have displaced traditional church activities, such as dealing with domestic prob-

issues the national identity/voter registration cards (*cédulas*) that are required identification for many financial and legal transactions.

Abstention rates, calculated as the proportion of registered voters who do not vote, was 32.8 percent in 1953 and 35.3 percent in 1958. These rates have declined since 1962, when much of the 1948 opposition returned to electoral politics and compulsory voting laws took effect. Since then, abstention rates have been relatively constant, varying between 17 and 21 percent (Tribunal Supremo de Elecciones 1986). Seligson found that the strongest predictor of electoral participation is party identification with the National Liberation Party (Partido Liberación Nacional—PLN) (Seligson 1987, 172). The PLN has the strongest, continuous electoral presence, which helps explain why PLN supporters would be more likely to vote. Geographically, those in less developed rural areas are least likely to vote, probably because of the time and expense of traveling to voting sites.[9] Banana zones also have lower than average voter turnout. Seligson explains that by migrating from their place of residence (where they are registered to vote) to work, banana workers become effectively disenfranchised (Seligson 1987, 173).

Despite numerous studies attempting to discover the socioeconomic correlates that explain party votes, historical party loyalties, most likely dating from the civil war of 1948, remain the most important factor (Seligson 1987).

Elections

The first elections held under the new constitution resulted in a landslide victory for José "Pepe" Figueres, running under the banner of the newly formed PLN. Since then, Costa Rica has held eleven consecutive, competitive, honest elections. From 1948 to 1970, control of the executive alternated every four years between the PLN and various opposition parties. From 1970 to 1978 and then again from 1982 to 1990, the PLN retained control of the executive for two consecutive terms. In 1990 the PLN lost to a united opposition, but in 1994 the party recaptured the presidency.

Until 1983, the opposition coalitions united disparate groups including the traditional oligarchy, some labor organizations, and the Calderonists (Salazar and Salazar 1992, 100–102, 144–46). Only when united is the opposition (anti-PLN) able to triumph over the PLN. The creation of a unified opposition party in 1983 and its electoral victory in 1990, discussed below, may signal a critical change in this electoral pattern.

The central dynamic in all elections since 1953 has been the contest be-

Table 5.2. *Representation of the PLN and Opposition Party (or Coalition) in the Costa Rican Assembly*

Year	President	PLN (%)	Opposition (%)	Others (%)
1953	Figueres	65	21	14
1958	Echandi	44	24	32
1962	Orlich	51	33	16
1966	Trejos	51	47	2
1970	Figueres	56	39	5
1974	Oduber	47	28	25
1978	Carazo	44	47	9
1982	Monge	58	32	10
1986	Arias	51	44	5
1990	Calderón	44	51	5
1994	Figueres	49	44	7

Source: Wilson (1992); Tribunal Supremo de Elecciones (1994).

the coalitions often shared only anti-PLN sentiments and not a legislative agenda (Rovira 1988, 34–45). This lack of cohesion benefited the PLN, making opposition presidents unable to effectively challenge the PLN political agenda. The dramatic changes in this project, discussed below, were undertaken by PLN governments rather than the opposition.[10]

Costa Rican elections are held every four years to choose simultaneously the president, legislators, and municipal governments. The president is elected directly, and deputies are elected by proportional representation from seven multimember districts (provinces), a division designed to guarantee representation to all parts of the country. In legislative elections, voters cast their vote for the party rather than a candidate, and the parties control the list of candidates in each region. Owing to the lack of residency requirements for the deputies and the parties' control over the list and the deputies' political careers, few incentives exist for effective geographic representation. Deputies are eligible for reelection, although not for consecutive terms. These provisions make the development of expertise and commitment to a career as a legislator difficult. In addition, candidates for the presidency cannot spend the

The PLN continues to call itself a "social democratic" party, advocating state-led economic growth, social welfare guarantees, and redistributive economic policies. Early party intellectuals, such as Rodrigo Facio, advocated "constructive" or interventionist liberalism (Romero 1977, 138, 225). Many observers, pointing to the absence of close ties to organized labor, the lack of commitment to reordering of the social and political system, and the denial of electoral rights to the Communist Party, see the PLN as predominately liberal or neoliberal. In an early analysis, Bodenheimer (1970, 87) argues that the PLN ideology remains very much within the liberal tradition and represents an eclectic attempt to find the "common developmental component within the unscientific Socialist, social Christian, Liberal and CEPAL tradition." Others have labeled the PLN as a bourgeois or middle-class reformist movement that lacks not only working-class structural support but also ideological coherence (Cerdas 1983).

Until the economic crisis of the 1980s, the PLN was committed to extensive state intervention in the economy and progressive social welfare measures. Since then, the shifting *tendencias* (factions) within the party represent a wide ideological spectrum, from social democrats to a clearly neoliberal wing (Rojas Bolaños 1992, 19). The internal structure of the PLN historically provided very few opportunities for participation by rank-and-file members.[12] Party members only began voting in party primaries to choose the presidential candidates in the 1980s. Recent reforms allow for the election of more party officials, and in 1997 the PLN plans to give up its traditional control of the party list and implement direct, secret elections in each province to choose candidates for the National Assembly (Prieto J. 1992; Rojas Bolaños 1992, 23).

Until Oscar Arias won the PLN nomination and then the presidency in 1986, the PLN was dominated by members of the Liberación Junta of 1948–49, such as Figueres (1953–58, 1970–74), Francisco Orlich (1962–66), Daniel Oduber (1974–78), and Luis Alberto Monge (1982–86). Oscar Arias Sánchez (1986–90) and Figueres's son, José María Figueres Olsen (1994–98), represent a new generation within the PLN.

Family connections appear to play an important role in the leadership of both parties. Thirty-four of the forty-four presidents from 1821 to 1976 were related to one of three elite families (Arias 1976). More recently, Rafael Angel Calderón Fornier, who is the son of former president Calderón Guardia (1940–48), won the presidency in 1990. The son of former president Trejos (Juan José Trejos Fonseca—PUSC) and the wife of former president Arias (Margarita Peñon—PLN) both ran unsuccessfully for the presidential nomination of their parties in 1993. Finally, José María Figueres Olsen, son of President José "Pepe" Figueres (1953–58, 1970–74), won the presidential election in 1994.

Bulgarelli 1992).[13] President Monge indicated that the consolidation of the opposition would serve as a challenge and stimulus for the PLN and the party system as a whole, strengthen democracy by lessening factionalism, and build a classic two-party system (Carballo Q. 1992; Aguilar Bulgarelli 1992). The PUSC triumphed in the elections of 1990, both winning control of the executive and, for the first time in Costa Rican history, securing an absolute majority in the assembly.

The unity of the opposition represents a consolidation of a two-party system in Costa Rica, a development that may have critical consequences for the stability of the regime. The strengthening of the opposition has not been accompanied by political polarization but rather by a diminished ideological distance between the two parties (Rovira 1992, 447–48; Vega Carballo 1991, 209). Combined with diminishing support for leftist parties, the unity of opposition parties strengthens the center of the political spectrum, a center that now includes almost 95 percent of the electorate (Vega Carballo 1991, 209). Lijphart's study (1984) of twenty-four democracies found that a low level of party polarization is important for maintaining democratic stability.

Evidence for the consolidation of a two-party system can be found in both national and municipal elections. The share of the electorate captured by the two major parties in presidential, congressional, and municipal elections has been steadily increasing since 1974 (see Vega 1992, 333). In 1990 the two parties obtained 98.67 percent of the presidential votes, 94.93 percent of the votes for the National Assembly, and 96.57 percent of the votes cast in municipal elections (TSE 1990). In 1994 the percentage of votes received by the major parties did decline somewhat. Most important, regional parties made significant gains in municipal elections. For example, in Limón, a province traditionally dissatisfied with its lack of representation and neglect by the national government, the Partido Agrario Nacional won a seat in the National Assembly and seats in each of the municipal governments in Limón province.

Left

The first leftist party in Costa Rica was organized by Jorge Volio in 1924. Advocating progressive social legislation, Volio ran for president under the banner of the Partido Reformista (Reformist Party) and won a surprising 20.4 percent of the vote (Seligson 1987, 164). The first Communist Party was organized in 1929 and slowly gained electoral and organizational strength. In 1943 the Communists, now called the Partido Vanguardia Popular, supported Calderón, who won the 1944 elections. After the civil war, the governing junta declared the Partido Vanguardia Popular illegal, and it was banned from

1869, and in 1973 the number of obligatory years of education was raised from six to nine (Rojas 1992, 98–99).[15] In addition, 93 percent of both males and females are literate (World Bank 1990, 219). Twenty-seven percent of the college-age population is enrolled in higher education, a rate that matches that of some advanced industrial countries.[16] Perhaps the most remarkable achievement during this period is the redistribution of income from the highest income sectors to the middle sectors.[17] Few documented cases of such redistribution can be found in the world, no others in Latin America.

In the early 1980s, Costa Rica suffered a severe and protracted economic crisis. A combination of declining terms of trade, sharp hikes in the price of oil and credit, and misguided domestic policies led Costa Rica to be the first country to declare a debt moratorium.[18] Costa Rica became one of the largest debtors (on a per capita basis) in the world.

In the face of the economic crisis, and under pressure from international lending agencies, Costa Rica has adopted a series of neoliberal economic reforms including privatization of some state enterprises and trade and monetary liberalization.[19] In response to drastic increases in utility rates, cuts in agricultural subsidies, and consumer price liberalization, new organizations emerged to resist the changes. These groups include peasant unions, public-sector unions, and urban groups protesting housing conditions and services.[20] From 1950 to 1980, agricultural cooperatives, neighborhood associations, development initiatives, and numerous governmental agencies were created by the government to address the needs of the population. As the financial capacity of the government to create and fund these institutions diminished in the 1980s, many resisted the changes. Since these groups have not been represented within the main political parties (Rovira 1992), their tactics were not confined to the electoral arena. Unions have taken their grievances to court, often winning wage concessions despite strong executive opposition. Numerous groups demanded attention by participating in an unprecedented number of strikes and protests between 1980 and 1988 (see Valverde et al. 1991). The government responded by opening negotiations and promising change. However, in the long run the promises have largely gone unfulfilled.[21] One example of unfulfilled promises is the dramatic cuts in agricultural subsidies and government services for small farmers, especially farmers producing for internal markets (Mora 1992).

As Seligson and Gómez B. (1989) argued in the first edition of *Elections and Democracy in Central America*, the severity of Costa Rica's economic crisis put the democratic system to the test. Surveys conducted before, during, and after the crisis reveal that Costa Ricans maintained high levels of support for their governmental institutions.[22] In the electoral arena, elections during the

This institutional innovation and adaptation suggest that democratic procedures will remain at the center of the Costa Rican political system.

The fact that Costa Rican democracy survived the economic crisis, its most difficult test yet, is remarkable. During the worst economic crisis of its history, despite unprecedented inflation, unemployment, and popular unrest, Costa Rica held regular, honest elections, consolidated two-party rule, and maintained high levels of popular support in its governmental institutions. Costa Rica's institutionalized democratic practices have demonstrated not only resiliency but also the capacity to adapt.

Notes

This chapter was written with support from the Institute for the Study of World Politics, the Social Science Research Council, Fulbright, and the Inter-American Foundation. I would like to thank Hugo Murillo Jiménez, Jorge Rovira Mas, Andrew Valls, Mitchell A. Seligson, John A. Booth, and an anonymous reviewer for their comments and suggestions.

1. See Dahl and Tufte (1973), Jackman (1975), and Seligson (1987) for a more complete discussion of the literature on size, development, and democracy.

2. Costa Rica consistently ranks as high as Western European democracies in evaluations conducted by Freedom House and Fitzgibbon-Johnson (Freedom House 1990; Wilkie and Ochoa 1989).

3. For attempts to explain democracy in Costa Rica, see Rodríguez Vega (1953), Kantor (1960), Pacheco (1961), Busey (1962), Aguilar Bulgarelli (1970), López Gutiérrez (1975), Arias Sánchez (1976), Stone (1979), Zelaya et al. (1979), Booth (1984), Peeler (1985), Seligson (1987), and Lehoucq (1990).

4. Seligson (1987) provides an extensive analysis of the attempts to establish constitutional rule in Costa Rica as well as the development of parties and elections.

5. Until the 1870s, the military leaders in Costa Rica were allied with civilian families.

6. Gudmundson (1986, 4) argues that municipal government provided a forum for peasant participation even in the nineteenth century, when popular participation in national politics was severely limited. The restrictions on geographic mobility in a country as mountainous and rugged as Costa Rica have always limited participation by the rural population.

7. The constitution originally permitted presidents to be reelected, but not to consecutive terms. A 1969 amendment prohibits presidents elected after that year from seeking reelection. José "Pepe" Figueres is the only president to serve two terms (1953–58 and 1970–74).

8. This trend appears to be especially strong in the 1980s. Gutiérrez (1992, 364–70) presents data comparing the number of laws approved by the legislature and those decreed by the executive. The centralization of power in the hands of the executive and the inefficiency of legislative power are common criticisms of the Costa Rican system. Even former presidents agree that the dominance of the president creates problems (see, for example, ANFE 1984, 7).

for Social Research that analyzed popular mobilization and government response from 1980 to 1988 (see Valverde, Pierre, and Araya 1992). For a summary of the largest strikes and protests, see Rojas Bolaños (1992).

22. There was some change in levels of system support between 1978 and 1980, but declines in support were almost all shifts from high to medium support. Critically, the proportion of cases exhibiting high system support was larger in 1983 than prior to the crisis in 1978 (Seligson and Muller 1987, 319–20).

23. More recent research reported in Booth's introductory chapter in this volume suggests levels of cultural support for democratic liberties among other Central American populations considerably greater than previously expected. In some cases support for democratic liberties elsewhere in the isthmus appeared by the early 1990s to equal or exceed those in Costa Rica.

References

Aguilar Bulgarelli, Oscar. 1970. "Fundamentos democráticos del sistema político costarricense." *Revista de ciencias sociales*, no. 7.
——. 1977. *Democracia y partidos políticos de Costa Rica*. San José, Costa Rica: Imprenta Lil.
——. 1991. *La constitución de 1949*. San José, Costa Rica: Editorial Costa Rica.
——. 1992. "Una nueva vía social-cristiana." In *El nuevo rostro de Costa Rica*, edited by Juan Manuel Villasuso, 287–312. Heredia, Costa Rica: Centro de Estudios Democráticos de América Latina.
Ameringer, Charles D. 1982a. "Costa Rica." In *Political Parties of the Americas, Canada, Latin America, and the West Indies*, edited by Robert J. Alexander, vol. 1. Westport, Conn.: Greenwood Press.
——. 1982b. *Democracy in Costa Rica*. New York: Praeger.
Araya Pochet, Carlos. 1969. *Historia de los partidos políticos: Liberación Nacional*, San José, Costa Rica: Editorial Costa Rica.
Arias Sánchez, Oscar. 1976. *¿Quién gobierna en Costa Rica?* San José, Costa Rica: Editorial Porvenir.
——. 1987. *Grupos de presión en Costa Rica*. San José, Costa Rica: Editorial Costa Rica.
Asociación Nacional de Fomento Económico (ANFE), ed. 1984. *El modelo político costarricense*. San José, Costa Rica: Asociación Nacional de Fomento Económico.
Bodenheimer, Susanne. 1970. "The Social Democratic Ideology in Latin America: The Case of Costa Rica's Partido Liberación Nacional." *Caribbean Studies* 10, no. 3.
Booth, John A. 1984. "Representative Constitutional Democracy in Costa Rica: Adaptation to Crisis in the Turbulent 1980s." In *Central America: Crisis and Adaptation*, edited by Steve C. Ropp and James A. Morris. Albuquerque: University of New Mexico Press.
——. 1989. "Elections and Democracy in Central America: A Framework for Analysis." In *Elections and Democracy in Central America*, edited by John A. Booth and Mitchell A. Seligson, 7–39. Chapel Hill: University of North Carolina Press.
——. 1990. "Costa Rica: The Roots of Democratic Stability." In *Politics in Developing Countries: Comparing Experiences with Democracy*, edited by Larry Diamond, Juan J. Linz, and Seymour Martin Lipset. Boulder, Colo.: Lynne Rienner.
——. 1993. "Costa Rican Democracy." In *Political Culture and Democracy in Developing Countries*, edited by Larry Diamond. Boulder, Colo.: Lynne Rienner.
Busey, James L. 1962. *Notes on Costa Rican Democracy*. Boulder: University of Colorado Press.
Carballo Q., Manuel. 1992. "El Partido Liberación Nacional: Necesidad de nuevos contenidos y formas de acción política." In *El nuevo rostro de Costa Rica*, edited by Juan Manuel Villasuso, 313–22. Heredia, Costa Rica: Centro de Estudios Democráticos de América Latina.
CCCS (*Cuadernos centroamericanos de ciencias sociales*). 1981. Issue no. 8, "Crisis en Costa Rica: Un debate." San José, Costa Rica: Confederación Superior Universitaria Centroamericana.
Cerdas, Rodolfo. 1983. "Costa Rica: Problemas actuales de una revolución democrática." In *¿Democ-*

Muñoz, Hugo Alfonso. 1981. *La asamblea legislativa en Costa Rica*. San José, Costa Rica: Editorial Costa Rica.

Nelson, Joan M. 1990. "The Politics of Adjustment in Small Democracies: Costa Rica, the Dominican Republic, Jamaica." In *Economic Crisis and Policy Choice: The Politics of Adjustment in Developing Countries*. Princeton: Princeton University Press.

Pacheco, Leon. 1961. "Evolución del pensamiento democrático." *Revista Combate* 15.

Peeler, John A. 1985. *Latin American Democracies*. Chapel Hill: University of North Carolina Press.

Prieto J., Marcelo. 1992. "Cambios en las organizaciones políticas costarricenses." In *El nuevo rostro de Costa Rica*, edited by Juan Manuel Villasuso, 277–86. Heredia, Costa Rica: Centro de Estudios Democráticos de América Latina.

Rodríguez Vega, Eugenio. 1953. *Apuntes para una sociología costarricense*. San José: Editorial de la Universidad de Costa Rica.

Rojas, Manuel, and Alvaro Fernández. 1991. *Contribuciones #13: Para entender las elecciones de 1990*. San José: Universidad de Costa Rica.

Rojas, Yolanda M. 1992. "Transformaciones recientes en la educación costarricense." In *El nuevo rostro de Costa Rica*, edited by Juan Manuel Villasuso, 97–122. Heredia, Costa Rica: Centro de Estudios Democráticos de América Latina.

Rojas Bolaños, Manuel. 1992. *Los años ochenta y el futuro incierto*. San José, Costa Rica: Editorial Universidad Estatal a Distancia.

Romero, Jorge Enrique. 1977. *La social democracia en Costa Rica*. San José, Costa Rica: Editorial Trejos Hermanos.

Rovira Mas, Jorge. 1988. *Estado y política económica en Costa Rica, 1948–1970*. San José, Costa Rica: Editorial Porvenir.

——. 1989. *Costa Rica en los años ochenta*. San José, Costa Rica: Editorial Porvenir.

——. 1992. "El nuevo estilo nacional de desarrollo." In *El nuevo rostro de Costa Rica*, edited by Juan Manuel Villasuso. Heredia, Costa Rica: Centro de Estudios Democráticos de América Latina.

Saborio, Sylvia. 1990. "Central America." In *Latin American Adjustment: How Much Has Happened?*, edited by John Williamson. Washington, D.C.: Institute for International Economics.

Salazar Mora, Orlando, and Jorge Mario Salazar Mora. 1992. *Los partidos políticos de Costa Rica*. San José, Costa Rica: Editorial Universidad Estatal a Distancia.

Sartori, Giovanni. 1976. *Parties and Party Systems: A Framework for Analysis*. Cambridge: Cambridge University Press.

Seligson, Mitchell A. 1980. *Peasants of Costa Rica and the Development of Agrarian Capitalism*. Madison: University of Wisconsin Press.

——. 1983. "Costa Rica." In *Latin America and Caribbean Contemporary Record, Volume I: 1981–1982*, edited by Jack W. Hopkins. New York: Holmes and Meier.

——. 1987. "Costa Rica and Jamaica." In *Competitive Elections in Developing Countries*, edited by Myron Weiner and Ergun Ozbudun. Durham, N.C.: Duke University Press.

——. 1990. "Costa Rica." In *Latin American Politics and Development*, edited by Howard J. Wiarda and Harvey F. Kline. Boulder, Colo.: Westview Press.

Seligson, Mitchell A., and Miguel Gómez B. 1989. "Ordinary Elections in Extraordinary Times: The Political Economy of Voting in Costa Rica." In *Elections and Democracy in Central America*, edited by John A. Booth and Mitchell A. Seligson, 158–84. Chapel Hill: University of North Carolina Press.

Seligson, Mitchell A., and Edward N. Muller. 1987. "Democratic Stability and Economic Crisis: Costa Rica, 1978–1983." *International Studies Quarterly* 31.

Schifter, Jacobo. 1979. *La fase oculta de la Guerra Civil en Costa Rica*. San José, Costa Rica: Editorial Universitaria Centroamericana.

Steichen, Regine. 1992. "Cambios en la orientación política-ideológica de los partidos políticos en la década de los 80." In *El nuevo rostro de Costa Rica*, edited by Juan Manuel Villasuso, 265–76. Heredia, Costa Rica: Centro de Estudios Democráticos de América Latina.

Stone, Samuel. 1976. *La dinastía de los conquistadores: La crisis del poder en la Costa Rica contemporánea*. San José, Costa Rica: Editorial Universitaria Centroamericana.

ELECTIONS UNDER CRISIS: BACKGROUND TO PANAMA IN THE 1980S

6

Orlando J. Pérez

This chapter examines the electoral trajectory of Panama's emerging democracy during the 1980s and 1990s. Panama, more than any country of the region, has experienced an uneven process of democratic transition. Elections were held throughout the 1980s, but the influence and control of the military and the intervention of the United States made the competitiveness and transparency of the electoral processes highly questionable.

The chapter analyzes the historical factors that have shaped the development of Panamanian politics throughout this century, factors that have hindered the establishment of a democratic regime. It analyzes the nature of the military government that ruled Panama from 1968 until the U.S. military invasion of 1989. The chapter looks at the electoral processes of 1984 and 1989 and why they failed as a mechanism of democratic consolidation. It concludes with an examination of the 1994 elections and their significance for the consolidation of a democratic regime.

Background: Panama's History

Five factors have shaped the nature of politics and society in Panama since the colonial period. First, the predominance of the transit route shaped the nature of the Panamanian economy. Panama's economy has been tied to the transfer of goods across the narrow stretch of the isthmus, affecting the behavior and values of elites as well as the institutional structures of the state. Second, the influence of the United States has served to condition political behavior in the isthmus. The United States was instrumental in developing the transit route

The ruling elite relied instead on extraterritorial powers to establish and maintain effective control.

The following periodization will help us to organize and understand Panamanian politics during this century. First, the period between 1903 and 1931 was characterized by the hegemonic rule of the Liberal Party; during the first ten years this rule was exercised in alliance with the Conservative Party. Second, between 1931 and 1968, Panamanian politics was characterized by the emergence of a middle class and populist movement led by Arnulfo Arias that challenged the hegemony of the Liberal Party and the commercial elite that controlled it. Third, from 1968 to 1981, politics was dominated by the National Guard with the help of a multiclass alliance. By 1981, with the death of General Omar Torrijos in a plane crash, the multiclass alliance began to break down with the emergence of old rivalries and partisan divisions. The death of Torrijos opens a fourth period, which was to last until the U.S. military invasion on December 20, 1989. The invasion marked the beginning of a fifth period, which is still ongoing. The period marks the return of civilian control of the government, continued fragmentation of political competition, and the attempt to consolidate a democratic regime.

1903–1931: The Hegemonic Rule of the Liberal Party

The new Panamanian state created on November 3, 1903, resulted from the convergence of diverse and complex factors that favored the interests of U.S. and Panamanian elites.[1] What emerged during the early twentieth century was a new alliance between Panamanian elites and Canal Zone officials, whose interests centered around the need for stability. The commercial elites, who dominated both the Conservative and Liberal Parties, lacked the economic basis on which to construct stable political power. The commercial elite did not control the principal component (i.e., the Panama Canal) of the service-oriented economy. The relationship with the United States (which did control the canal) served as a surrogate for maintaining the authority of the state (Ropp 1982; Lafeber 1989).

The early period of the republic was dominated by the Liberal Party. The Liberal Party has deep roots within Panamanian society going back to the beginning of the nineteenth century (Soler 1976, 1985, 1988). The party reflected the commercial interests concentrated in the cities of Panama and Colón, as well as those of small and medium agricultural producers. The alliance between the urban commercial class and the small agricultural pro-

1931–1968: Emergent Nationalism and the
Dominance of Arnulfo Arias

By the late 1920s, the impact of the Great Depression served to exacerbate tensions between Panamanians and the United States. Panamanians found themselves competing for unskilled jobs on the "silver roll" with West Indian blacks, whose forefathers had been imported by the U.S. Panamanian Canal Company to supply manual labor for canal construction.[2] Panamanians now condemned the foreigner—whether U.S. technician or West Indian laborer— as an invader who seized the profits of the international waterway while Panamanians suffered economic deprivation (Lewis 1980; de Lewis 1979; Maloney and Priestly 1975).

The ill effects of the depression were especially acute in the terminal cities of Panama and Colón. In these ports lived the emerging middle class of Panama, who depended on the commercial prosperity of the canal for their livelihood. Most of these middle-class groups had migrated from rural to urban areas, where they had managed to acquire the rudiments of an education and had entered business or government service. As much as the unemployed Panamanian who competed with blacks in the Canal Zone, the middle classes of Panama City and Colón resented U.S. policy in Panama and sought greater commercial benefits from the canal. Similarly, these elements were xenophobic, expressing hostility toward the encroachment of Anglo-Saxon norms in isthmian life.

Isthmian nationalism found expression in the Acción Comunal (precursor of the Panameñista movement) coup of 1931. Founded in 1926, Acción Comunal represented an important opposition to the Liberal presidency of Florencio Harmodio Arosemena, whom it accused of having organized electoral fraud to capture the executive office. The basic ideological tenants of Acción Comunal were nationalist and fervently anti–United States. The slogan adopted by the organization was *"Patriotismo, Acción, Equidad y Disciplina"* (Patriotism, Action, Equality, and Discipline) (Beluche Mora 1981).

By 1931, accusations of corruption and political scandals involving Arosemena reached a high pitch. On January 2, Acción Comunal launched a coup that successfully unseated the Panamanian president. After the coup a transitional government was established to rule until the elections of 1932. The elections were won by Harmodio Arias, brother of Arnulfo Arias, the leader of Acción Comunal and founder of the Panameñista movement.

In 1940 Arnulfo Arias founded the National Revolutionary Party, partisan expression of the Panameñista movement. His program called for a new

regime to gain a certain level of autonomy from societal actors was conducive to the long-term survival of the regime. Steve Ropp argues that the military's ability to directly and indirectly extract economic resources from Panama's large service sector was a deciding factor in maintaining it in power (1992, 212). The resources obtained through the monopolization of the quasi-licit and illicit activities of the service sector allowed the military institution to maintain its own independence and to partially subsidize the "popular bureaucracy" that served as its political power base within the larger structure of the authoritarian regime.[8]

The military was also able to distribute selective incentives to the traditional ruling commercial class. The expansion of the Colón Free Trade Zone and the growth in the International Banking Center were aimed at guaranteeing the viability of the service-oriented economy on which the economic interests of the commercial class depended.[9] The commercial class also took advantage of the illicit activities sponsored by the National Guard (Ropp 1992).[10]

In 1978, after ten years of governance, Torrijos announced a "return to the barracks." The role of both the National Legislative Council and the National Assembly of Representatives was modified to reflect the desire of the regime to impart a more liberal democratic appearance to the institutions of government.[11] In a further effort to promote "liberalization," political parties were once again legalized, and the regime formed its own party, the Revolutionary Democratic Party (Partido Revolucionario Democrático—PRD) (Gandásegui H. 1989, 29; Soler Torrijos 1993, 150–51; Materno Vásquez 1987b, 239–41).

1981–1989: The End of the Liberalization Process and the Emergence of Noriega

Panama's post-1969 period of political stability ended with the sudden death of Torrijos on July 30, 1981. After some skillful maneuvering, deceit, and positive support from the United States, Manuel Antonio Noriega emerged as the maximum leader of the National Guard in August 1983, which he promptly expanded and upgraded into the Panamanian Defense Forces (*La Prensa*, September 8, 9, and 11, 1983).

The liberalization program of Torrijos had envisioned presidential elections in 1984. In 1983 the successor government dominated by Manuel Noriega promoted a set of constitutional reforms that would seemingly have further adapted the structures of the Panamanian state to that of a liberal democracy (Pedreschi 1991, 715–20; Ricord 1991, 753–68).

The government supported the candidacy of Nicolas Ardito Barletta (vice president of the World Bank) under the premise that he could assure the flow of international investment capable of counteracting the economic recession the country was suffering (Gandásegui H. 1989, 72; Arias de Para 1984, 24–26). The government candidate was supported by the Revolutionary Democratic Party, the Labor Party, the Republican Party, the Liberal Party, and the Revolutionary Panameñista Party, forming the National Democratic Union (UNADE). The opposition forces coalesced into the Democratic Opposition Alliance (ADO), composed of the Authentic Panameñista Party, the Christian Democratic Party, and the Liberal Republican Nationalist Movement and headed by the octogenarian Arnulfo Arias, who was making his last run for the presidency (Espino Z. 1987; Conte Porras 1990, 488–89, 518; Gandásegui H. 1989, 72–73).

The elections of 1984 were plagued with irregularities, and the opposition charged that only fraud could explain the victory of the official candidate (Arias de Para 1984).[12] The United States, however, supported the victory of the government candidate. The U.S. secretary of state, George Shultz, backed the election of Nicolas Ardito Barletta by traveling to Panama for the presidential inauguration (Dinges 1990, 196–99).

The relations between Panama and the United States rapidly deteriorated after the honeymoon that followed the election of Ardito Barletta. The president did not control the National Assembly, which made difficult the passage of his legislative initiatives, nor did he exercise influence over the Defense Forces, which advanced their own political program, independent of the executive.

As a consequence, President Barletta could not get approval for his structural adjustment program demanded by the International Monetary Fund (IMF). He also could not assure the cooperation of the Panamanian Defense Forces in the military adventures of the United States in Central America. In September 1985, Ardito Barletta was forced to resign, engendering a distancing between the United States and Panama.[13]

Under the presidency of Eric A. Delvalle, imposed thereafter by the Panamanian Defense Forces (PDF), the political deterioration continued. The comfortable relationship between the commercial and industrial elite and the National Guard that had secured the stability of the regime came to an end in the mid-1980s as Noriega began to expand his reach. The military went from an intermediary organization capable of negotiating with all social classes to imposing its vision of Panama on all sectors of society. Noriega saw the military as the inheritor of the U.S. role in the isthmus. He increased the military capabilities of the National Guard, centralized power within his office, and renamed it the Panamanian Defense Forces.[14] All this was done, according to

Duque, a friend and business collaborator of General Noriega (Martínez H. 1990, 149–58; Dinges 1990; Koster and Sánchez 1990; Scranton 1991).

The elections centered around opposition to the Noriega-led regime. The forces of ADOC emphasized their antimilitarism and advocated the establishment of a liberal democratic system. The Coalición Liberal Nacionalista emphasized national sovereignty and opposition to U.S. aggression. In the end, the elections were devoid of any real ideological or programmatic content. Both sides, except for being in favor of "nationalism" or "democracy," said little about what actual programs they would implement if elected.

In the early morning hours of May 8 and throughout that day, partial results from three electoral districts were published. The results favored the government candidates. While the government published the partial results it received from the National Counting Board, the church announced the results it was given by the opposition. The differences were significant. While the government claimed their candidates had a two-to-one majority in the electoral districts that had been counted, the opposition announced a landslide victory for its candidates. Figure 6.2 represents the results as compiled by the Catholic Church. The figures were subsequently published by the Committee for the Support of External Observers. After the 1989 U.S. invasion, the new government used these figures to legitimize its electoral victory.

On May 9 the flow of information from the district to the national level was interrupted, and on the 10th the president of the Electoral Tribunal read a statement signed by all three magistrates annulling the elections. The statement alluded to the fact that the great number of irregularities across the country made counting the votes impossible. The communiqué also mentioned the open involvement of the United States in the elections.

In the demonstrations that ensued, several opposition candidates were badly beaten up by the PDF, with the images captured and broadcast on television throughout the world. The Organization of American States (OAS) immediately and strongly condemned the actions of the Noriega regime. Negotiations sponsored by the OAS between the two factions failed. Noriega refused to negotiate and insisted that any talks had to take place between the civilian leaders of the regime and the opposition. In reality, neither side had any incentive to negotiate in good faith. Both believed that the United States was on their side and would come to their rescue. Noriega never believed that the U.S. opposition was serious or that it would lead where it did. The civilian opposition believed that in the end the United States would get rid of Noriega for them (Dinges 1990; Kempe 1990; Buckley 1991).

Nothing was done to remove Noriega from power until October 3, 1989, however. On that day, two hundred members of the Defense Forces mounted an attack on the Panamanian military headquarters. The attempted coup failed partly because the United States refused to intervene on behalf of the coup plotters (*La Estrella de Panama*, October 4, 5, and 6, 1989; *Critica*, October 6, 1989; Dinges 1990, 305–6).

After the failed coup, Noriega seemed stronger than ever. The domestic opposition had been defeated and neutralized, the U.S. sanctions had inflicted pain but failed to topple the regime, and the verbal condemnations from the OAS had no effect whatsoever. Noriega continued throughout November and December to challenge the United States, even going to the point of declaring "war." On December 20, 1989, the United States moved to remove Noriega from power by sending twenty thousand U.S. troops to invade Panama.

Postinvasion Politics

After the invasion, the Panamanian Defense Forces were dissolved, and their command was destroyed. Many of the civilian leaders that had supported the military regime were imprisoned, and others left the country. The new government had a huge majority (fifty-five of the sixty-seven seats) in the National Assembly and total U.S. support.

A major task of the new government installed after the invasion was the transformation of the military institution. The minister of government and justice at the time, Ricardo Arias Calderón, decided in February 1990 to replace the Defense Forces with a Public Force composed of three services: the National Police, the National Air Service, and the National Maritime Service. The decree that created these entities assigned them responsibility for public order and national defense and envisioned the possibility that special units with external defense functions might be created in the future. Yet these services were almost completely demilitarized in terms of their personnel, who were largely recruited from the former PDF. The new security forces were subordinated to civilian authorities through direct control by the Ministry of Government and Justice and budgetary oversight by the Office of the Comptroller General, as well as by the Legislative Assembly (*Gaceta Oficial* 1990).

These changes reflect significant advances over the previous national security model. One notable achievement has been the clear separation of state security agencies with distinct mandates for law enforcement, air rescue, coastal surveillance, criminal investigation, presidential security, and so on. The second major accomplishment has been the subordination of all state

Table 6.1. *Political Tolerance in Central America*

	Costa Rica (%)	El Salvador (%)	Guatemala (%)	Honduras (%)	Nicaragua (%)	Panama (%)
Right to vote:						
Disapprove	42.9	57.5	55.8	27.6	41.1	27.7
Approve	57.0	42.4	36.0	72.1	55.5	72.4
Don't know	0.2	0.1	8.3	0.4	3.4	0.4
Right to demonstrate:						
Disapprove	40.7	51.8	48.6	23.9	34.5	27.0
Approve	59.1	48.1	42.4	76.0	62.1	72.8
Don't know	0.2	0.1	9.1	0.2	3.4	0.2
Right to run for office:						
Disapprove	58.8	61.1	69.6	32.5	59.1	38.6
Approve	41.0	38.8	20.5	67.3	37.8	61.0
Don't know	0.2	0.1	10.0	0.2	3.1	0.4
Right to free speech:						
Disapprove	53.9	58.5	63.9	27.0	53.3	39.6
Approve	45.9	41.4	26.9	72.6	43.3	60.2
Don't know	0.2	0.1	9.2	0.4	3.4	0.2

Source: Booth (1993).

Note: Political tolerance is determined by four items measuring the extent to which the respondents are willing to grant these rights to political dissenters.

constantly criticize the political system; 86.2 percent firmly approved their right to protest peacefully; 86.2 percent firmly approved their right to run for public office; and 65.5 percent approved their right to make a speech on television.

The role of the military is another important issue for the ultimate survival of democracy. On this subject, 96.6 percent of elites interviewed said that nothing justified a military coup. When asked about the utility of the military for solving various national problems, vast majorities expressed the opinion that the military could not help to solve most of the major social, political, or economic problems facing the nation.

The task of constructing democratic institutions in Panama can count on other assets. The population is relatively well educated, with an adult literacy rate of 88 percent. More than 80 percent have access to health services and potable water. Although 14 percent of children suffer from malnutrition and 18 percent of the population is unable to satisfy basic needs, these figures are far lower than those in most of the region (*Central America Report* 1994). The

Table 6.2. *Presidential Election Results, May 8, 1994*

Candidates	Votes	%
Ernesto Pérez B.	355,307	33.3
Mireya de Gruber	310,372	29.1
Ruben Blades	182,405	17.1
Ruben Carles	171,192	16.1
Eduardo Vallarino	25,476	2.4
Samuel L. Galindo	18,424	1.7
José S. Muñoz	3,668	0.3
Total	1,066,844	100.0

Source: Electoral Tribunal.

ment, Papa Egoro, were a breath of fresh air for many Panamanians, who saw in the "outsider" the ability to clean up the system. Blades, however, could not overcome his late start and lack of organizational power in the countryside. The results of the elections favored the candidate of the Revolutionary Democratic Party (PRD), Ernesto Pérez Balladares. The PRD was founded in 1979 by the military regime to organize and lead the liberalization process begun that year. It was thought that the party had been destroyed after the 1989 U.S. invasion when many of its supporters and prominent leaders were put in jail. The party, however, was able to reorganize itself during the 1990s and came to represent the strongest opposition to the Endara government. With the government's popularity at its lowest point, the PRD capitalized on the feelings of frustration among Panama's citizens to win the presidency.

The constitution also requires that all candidates for the Legislative Assembly be on the lists of approved parties. In districts having only one legislator, a simple plurality is enough to win, but in others, such as Panama City, which elect several legislators, the final result is based on a complicated formula involving party lists and modified proportional representation. The result is to virtually guarantee a divided assembly in which the party that wins the presidency will have a minority of the total seats (see table 6.3).

Panama's 1994 election had a special importance, since the administration inaugurated in September 1994 will be responsible for managing the transfer of the canal and the military bases from the United States to Panama. Most Panamanians recognize that their success or failure in dealing with this transfer will play a determinant role in shaping the nation's economic and political

that the 1994 elections gave the public an opportunity, for the first time in many years, to freely choose the country's president, legislators, and local officials, the election expanded the range of political participation. This expansion, however, is the minimum required under a liberal democratic regime. Any further expansion of the range of political participation awaits the actions of the next government.

The breadth of political participation refers to the fraction of the citizenry participating in making decisions. In the 1994 elections the voter turnout was 73.6 percent. Although electoral participation does not constitute a deep form of participation, it does reflect the high level of interest and legitimacy given to the electoral process. In the same urban survey mentioned earlier, 45.9 percent of respondents said they had attempted to convince others how to vote.[22] In addition, 29.3 percent said they worked for a political candidate, and 22.9 percent attended professional association meetings sometimes or frequently. Overall, Panama ranked the second highest (behind Honduras) of political participation among the five nations surveyed during 1991.

The depth of political participation refers to the extent to which participation can truly influence public decisions and it is autonomous. To the extent that the 1994 electoral decision was free of fraud and manipulation from the government or other forces (external and internal), at least at the election level, the depth of participation has increased. It remains to be seen, however, if such increase extends to other levels of participation, levels that are far more important to the ultimate consolidation of democracy.

The fourth question refers to the environment in which the elections were held. There can be little question that the 1994 elections were held in an environment conducive to the free exercise of participatory rights and that the conduct of the election was fair. The work of both the Electoral Tribunal and the executive helped to assure that the elections were held in such an environment. Moreover, the efforts of the church to commit the political parties to conduct themselves in a fair and clean manner during the campaign also helped to establish the proper environment for the realization of free and competitive elections.[23]

The last two questions, referring to the effects of the elections on the consolidation of a democratic system and on the establishment of a political culture of support for participation and democratic rules, are much more difficult to answer. To the extent that the 1994 elections are the beginning of a process in which the political participation of citizens extends beyond the mere act of voting to include important economic and social decisions, the elections would be a step forward. Moreover, if the problems of institutional gridlock are to be resolved, the relationship between the executive and the legislature

ning the transisthmian railroad. The United States had also showed an interest in building an interoceanic canal through Central America.

Coupled with these mutual concerns were the desires of Panamanian elites to exercise a greater degree of autonomy from the central government in Bogotá (it is important to note that at the time Panama was part of Colombia). Justo Arosemena, a leading Panamanian political figure of the time, advocated the establishment of a federal system that would give Panama more power over its internal affairs (Arosemena 1981). Panamanian elites felt their best interests lay with the building of an interoceanic canal that would allow them to exploit fully Panama's geographic position and with greater internal autonomy. Those two factors formed the basis of the alliance between the United States and Panamanian elites. The alliance took shape in 1903 with the rejection by the Colombian Senate of the Herran-Hay Treaty, which would have built the canal through Panama while it remained part of Colombia. At the time, both the United States and Panamanian elites felt the only way to build the canal was to separate Panama from Colombia.

2. Payment for canal workers was divided between those paid in gold, who were on the "gold roll," and those paid in silver, who were on the "silver roll." The former was exclusively the domain of white, skilled jobs, whereas the latter was for "colored," unskilled laborers.

3. The 1941 constitution lasted until 1946, when a popularly elected National Constituent Assembly wrote a new, more progressive constitution.

4. In 1949, with the death of the president, the National Guard recounted the votes of the 1948 elections and declared that Arnulfo had won after all. He was then inaugurated president, only to be violently overthrown in 1951.

5. For accounts of the events of October 11, see Materno Vásquez (1987a, 1987b), Conte Porras (1980, 1990), Gandásegui H. (1989), Koster and Sánchez (1990), and Soler Torrijos (1993).

6. Boris Martínez was ousted in March 1969 for advocating "radical" reform programs (Gandásegui H. 1989, 38; Materno Vásquez 1987a, 87).

7. Bonapartism has been described as a semicompetitive system characterized by a strong executive, the lapse of control by the ruling class, and the painless demobilization of the subordinate and the dominant social strata. In such systems the repressive level is moderate, and the reforms set forth do not threaten the dominant property system. A Bonapartist state is unified by an ideology of "exalted nationalism." This type of regime exhibits a high degree of centralism maintained by the state bureaucracy.

8. The "popular bureaucracy" sector has been labeled the "dependent middle class." It is composed of lower- and middle-level government functionaries who owe their livelihood to the government and are easily incorporated into the support network (party members and contributors, as well as voters) of the regime.

9. The Colón Free Trade Zone was created in the 1950s and is composed of hundreds of commercial establishments dedicated to the export and reexport of duty-free items. In the 1970s, the military government relaxed the banking laws to encourage the establishment of banks and bank branches in Panama. Through the relaxed banking rules, Panama became a leading international banking center.

10. These activities included money laundering, drug trafficking, and the utilization of government contracts to favor certain "friends" of the National Guard.

11. Both the National Legislative Council and the National Assembly of Representatives were set up by the 1972 constitutional reforms. The first was envisioned as a consultative body to the executive branch, and the second was composed of local representatives elected within the smallest political divisions (i.e., the Corregimiento). Elections were nonpartisan.

Justice and Peace Commission. Out of those meetings emerged the Ethical and Moral Electoral Agreement, which committed all participants to an ethical conduct of their respective campaigns.

References

Arauz, Celestino Andres, Carlos Manuel Gateazoro, and Armando Muñoz. 1979. *La historia de Panamá en sus textos, tomo II, 1903–1968.* Panama City: Editorial Universitaria.

Arias de Para, Raul. 1984. *Así fue el fraude: Las elecciones presidenciales de Panamá, 1984.* 2d ed. Panama City: Imp. Edilito.

Arosemena, Justo. 1981. *Panamá y nuestra América.* Mexico City: UNAM.

Arosemena, Mariano. 1979. *Historia y nacionalidad.* Panama City: Editorial Universitaria.

Beluche Mora, Isidro. 1981. *Acción comunal, surgimiento y estructuración del nacionalismo panameño.* Panama City: Editorial Condor.

Berguido G., Fernando. 1987. *La sucesión presidencial en Panamá.* Panama City: Editorial La Antigua.

Bernal, Miguel Antonio. 1992. *Reformas o constituyente.* Panama City: Ediciones Nari.

Booth, John A. 1993. "Democracy in Central America: Deepening without Consolidation?" Paper delivered at the Conference on Deepening Democracy and Representation in Latin America, University of Pittsburgh, April 17–18.

Booth, John A., and Mitchell A. Seligson. 1989. *Elections and Democracy in Central America.* Chapel Hill: University of North Carolina Press.

Buckley, Kevin. 1991. *Panama: The Whole Story.* New York: Simon and Schuster.

Castillero Calvo, Alfredo. 1973. "Transitismo y dependencia: El caso del Istmo de Panamá." *Loteria* 210 (July): 17–40.

———. 1980. *Economía terciaria y sociedad: Panamá siglos XVI and XVII.* Panama City: Impresora de la Nacion.

———. 1983. *America Hispana: Aproximaciones a la historia económica.* Panama City: Impresora de la Nacion/INAC.

Castillero Pimentel, Ernesto. 1964. *Panamá y los Estados Unidos.* Panama City: Editora Panamá América.

Castillero Reyes, Ernesto. 1965. *Historia de Panamá.* Panama City: Editora Renovación.

Castro, Nils. 1974. *Justo Arosemena: Antiyanqui y latinoamericanista.* Panama City: Ministerio de Gobierno y Justicia.

Centro de Estudios y Acción Social Panameño (CEASPA). 1987. *Este pais mes a mes.* Boletín mensual. Panama City: CEASPA.

Central America Report. 1994. January 14.

Comité de Apoyo a los Observadores Internacionales. 1989. *Testimonio de un proceso electoral.* Edited by Jairo Mora F. Panama City: R. de Panamá.

Conte Porras, Jorge. 1980. *Arnulfo Arias Madrid.* Panama City: Litho Impresora Panamá, S.A.

———. 1990. *Requiem por la revolución.* San José, Costa Rica: Litografía e Imprenta Lil, S.A.

Cooley, John A. 1972. "The US and the Panama Canal, 1938–1947." Ph.D. diss., Ohio State University.

Cuestas Gómez, Carlos. 1992. *Soldados americanos en Chiriquí (La ocupación militar de 1918).* Panama City: Litografia Enan, S.A.

de Lewis, Catalina N. G. 1979. *Los trabajadores panameños de ascendencia antillana en la zona del canal de Panamá.* Panama City: CELA.

Delgado D., Daniel. 1988. "Fundamentos para la estrategia de defensa de la República de Panamá." *La República,* August 14.

de Souza, Herbert. 1976. "Notas acerca de la situación socio-política de Panamá." *Tareas* 35:7–42.

Dinges, John. 1990. *Our Man in Panama.* New York: Random House.

Duncan, Jeptha. 1921. *La educación publica en Panamá.* Panama City: Ministerio de Educación.

Sepulveda, Melinda. 1983. *Harmodio Arias Madrid: El hombre, el estadista, y el periódico*. Panama City: Editorial Universitaria.

Soler, Ricaurte. 1976. *Panamá, dependencia y liberación*. San José, Costa Rica: EDUCA.

———. 1985. *Formas ideológicas de la nación panameña*. Panama City: Ediciones Tareas.

———. 1987. *Panama: Nación y oligarquía*. Panama City: Ediciones Tareas.

———. 1988. *Pensamiento político en los siglos XIX y XX*. Panama City: Universidad de Panamá.

Soler Torrijos, Giancarlo. 1993. *La invasión a Panamá: Estrategias y tácticas para el nuevo orden mundial*. Panama City: CELA.

Wong, Guillermo J. 1988. "La defensa y la seguridad del Canal de Panamá." In *El futuro del Canal de Panamá*. Panama City: Fundación Omar Torrijos.

Zimbalist, Andrew, and John Weeks. 1991. *Panama at the Crossroads: Economic Development and Political Change in the Twentieth Century*. Berkeley and Los Angeles: University of California Press.

Zúñiga, Carlos Ivan. 1973. *El desarme de la policia nacional*. Panama City: Editorial Cart Patrioticas.

Newspapers

Gaceta Oficial (official government document)
La Prensa
La Estrella de Panamá
El Panamá América
Crítica

PART TWO: ISSUES

WHO VOTES IN CENTRAL AMERICA? A COMPARATIVE ANALYSIS

Mitchell A. Seligson, Annabelle Conroy,
Ricardo Córdova Macías, Orlando J. Pérez,
and Andrew J. Stein

In 1986, when the Latin American Studies Association (LASA) panel was held that produced the papers that were published in *Elections and Democracy in Central America* (Booth and Seligson 1989), competitive, free, and fair elections were the exception rather than the rule in Central America. Only Costa Rica had a long history of elections that, by any standard, were a model of electoral probity. As a result, very little was known then about the Central American voter, and therefore Costa Rica was the only country in that volume in which voting behavior was analyzed in any depth. This is not to say that the chapters did not make reference to elections and their results but to stress that it was not possible at that time to undertake a serious empirical analysis of voting behavior along the classical lines developed by political scientists in the United States and Western Europe.

Times have changed, however. Regular elections are beginning to become a normal feature of the Central American political landscape. As already noted, Costa Rica's elections have a long tradition, dating from the early part of the twentieth century, having been interrupted only once, in 1948. After the 1980 constituent assembly election, Honduras has had democratic presidential elections since 1981, with the Liberal Party winning in that year and again in 1985, to be defeated by the National Party in the 1989 election (Molina Chocano 1990; Navarro 1990). Guatemala began a formal transformation to civilian rule in 1984 with the election of a constituent assembly and since then has held competitive presidential elections in 1985 and 1990. In El Salvador, elections have

villages. For example, in some countries populations over twenty-five hundred are considered urban when, in fact, these places are at best no more than very small towns. We sought to narrow our definition of urban to include the areas of major population agglomeration. In Guatemala this meant Guatemala City, Esquintla, Quezaltenango, and other major concentrations. In El Salvador it meant greater metropolitan San Salvador, including the city of San Salvador (divided into fourteen zones) and the eight surrounding *municipios*: Soyapango, Cuscatancingo, Ciudad Delgado, Mejicanos, Nueva San Salvador, San Marcos, Ilopango, and Antiguo Cuscatlán. In Honduras it meant the nation's two large metropolitan areas, Tegucigalpa (the capital) and San Pedro Sula. In Nicaragua this definition included Managua (the capital) and the regional cities of León, Granada, and Masaya. In Costa Rica the sample covered the greater metropolitan region, incorporating San José (the nation's capital) and the provincial capitals of the *meseta central*—Cartago, Heredia, and Alajuela. Finally, the Panama sample was confined to the metropolitan Panama City area.

Country samples were of area probability design. In each country the most recent population census data were used. Within each stratum, census maps were used to select, at random, an appropriate number of political subdivisions (e.g., districts), and within each subdivision the census maps were used to select an appropriate number of segments from which to draw the interviews.[3] Within the household, all voting-age residents were eligible for selection, and one was chosen at random (using either the "next birthday system" or a sex/age quota system).

Costa Rica was established as the country for the pilot test of the survey items. That sample was gathered in the fall of 1990. The surveys in the other five countries were then carried out during the summer of 1991 and the winter of 1991–92. The design called for samples in the range of at least 500 to a maximum of 1,000 respondents from each country. The lower boundary of 500 respondents was established so as to provide a sufficient number of cases from each country to allow for reliable statistical analysis at the level of the country.[4] The sample sizes for each country are as follows: Guatemala, $N = 904$; El Salvador, $N = 910$; Honduras, $N = 566$; Nicaragua, $N = 704$; Costa Rica, $N = 597$; Panama, $N = 500$.

Turnout

Perhaps the two most basic parameters in any study of voting are turnout of eligible voters and turnout as a percentage of registered voters. Although at

We also recognized another limitation of survey data, namely that of over-reporting. According to voter validation studies conducted by the University of Michigan, survey data overreported voting by 18 percent in the 1970s in the United States (Katosh and Traugott 1981). Yet the rate of overreporting for Central America may be substantially lower. For example, Hernández R. (1991, 121), using official turnout results, found that 82 percent of all registered voters (calculated to be 96 percent of all eligible voters) cast a ballot in the 1986 election. In a 1987 national survey conducted by Seligson in Costa Rica, turnout was reported as 83 percent, only 1 percent above the actual rate.

These obstacles present formidable barriers to developing good estimates of turnout against which we can compare the survey data. Nonetheless, it is worth the effort to make these comparisons in order to have some idea as to how accurately our surveys represent these six nations. Table 7.1 provides the best data that we were able to develop. One of the major challenges was to obtain reasonable population estimates and then to calculate from those the voting-age population for the urban areas in which we conducted the surveys. Our survey data theoretically coincide most closely with the percentage of the voting-age population that voted rather than the turnout of registered voters. This is because we interviewed from a universe of all households, not just those in which the respondent was registered to vote. For completeness, however, we also provide the best data we could find on the number of registered voters for each country and city in which we conducted our study, as well as the turnout of registered voters in those cities.

How well did our survey results approximate our best estimate of the voting turn out? Theoretically, our confidence interval was as large as 4.5 percent for Panama and Honduras, where our sample was approximately 500, and as small as 3.3 percent in Guatemala and El Salvador, where our sample was approximately 900. In Costa Rica, where the percentage of the urban *meseta central* voting-age population that voted was 89 percent, our survey revealed 84 percent, with a confidence interval that would go as high as 87.3 percent. In Tegucigalpa, Honduras, we came even closer, with the survey showing 83 percent and the actual turnout 87 percent. Results in San Pedro Sula, Honduras, were not as close, exceeding by 7 percent the estimated actual totals (93 percent versus 86 percent). The survey was also quite close in Managua, Nicaragua, with the survey at 79 percent and the actual vote of 71 percent. In the other samples, our estimates were considerably higher than the actual vote. In Panama City, for example, our survey result was 78 percent, with a lower estimate of 73.5 percent, whereas the estimated actual vote was 64 percent. In El Salvador the estimate for the survey was 63 percent and the lower estimate a little over 59 percent, whereas the actual vote was 49 percent.

of Voting-Age Population That Voted	Number of Registered Voters (millions)	% of Registered Voters That Voted	Survey Results (%)	Voting Compulsory/ Not Compulsory
				compulsory
79	1.69	82	—	
89	0.60	82	84	
				compulsory
44	2.1	52	—	
49	0.45	73	63	
				compulsory (except illiterates,
41	3.20	57	—	invalids, and 70+ years)
40	0.62	63	70	
				compulsory
79	2.37	76	—	
87	0.35	75	83	
86	0.19	69	93	
				not compulsory
75	1.75	86	—	
71	0.38	88	79	
				not compulsory
55	1.19	63	—	
64	0.28	69	78	

and Tribunal Supremo Electoral, Centro de Asesoría y Promoción Electoral del Instituto Interamericano de Derechos Humanos (CAPEL/IIDH), *Informe final del programa de capacitación electoral 1990*, Guatemala: TSE/CAPEL, March 1991. Guatemala City population estimates from "Estimaciones de población urban y rural por Departamento y Municipio: 1990–1995" (Guatemala: Instituto Nacional de Estadísticas).

Honduras: "Censo nacional de población y vivienda, 1988: Características generales de la población y de las viviendas por barrios y colonias, San Pedro Sula y Tegucigalpa" (Tegucigalpa, December 1990); unpublished data, Tribunal Nacional de Elecciones. Note that the number of registered voters in Tegucigalpa, as given, is larger than the voting-age population. This may be a result of the underestimation of the voting-age population, estimates made from the CELADE population estimates or from differences in the way the area included in the population census for Tegucigalpa versus the voting districts included as part of the city.

Nicaragua: Data for Managua are for Region III, which includes Managua and the surrounding areas. No voting data are available for the city itself, but the population of the city of Managua was 903,620, whereas Region III had a population of 1,067,881. Hence, the city was 84.6 percent of the region. Latin American Studies Association, Commission to Observe the 1990 Nicaraguan Election, "Electoral Democracy under International Pressure," March 15, 1990, mimeo; "Cómo voto Nicaragua: Los resultados electorales," *Envío* (Managua-UCA) (April 1990): 1–24. Abstention rates of registered voters taken from Vanessa Castro and Gary Prevost, *The 1990 Elections in Nicaragua and Their Aftermath* (Lanham, Md.: Rowman and Littlefield, 1992), 223.

Panama: OEA (1992, 40). Results based on recount. Estimates of turnout vary from 54 to 75 percent. Our calculations, based on data from the Electoral Tribunal and reported by the Comité de Apoyo a

Figure 7.1. *Average Turnout of Eligible Voters: Central America in Comparative Perspective*

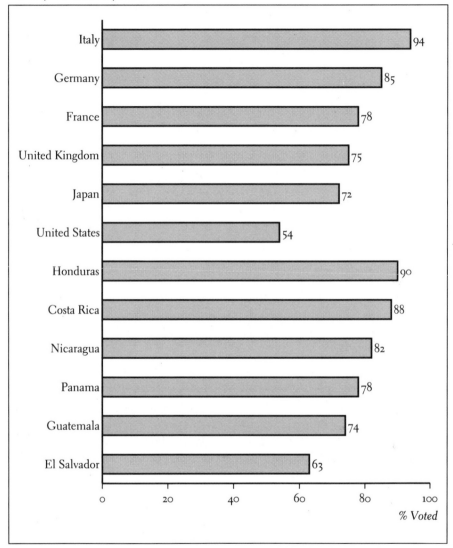

Source: University of Pittsburgh Central American Public Opinion Project; Powell (1986, 38).

since the urban and rural differentials are not nearly so great in these developed countries as they are in Central America. Wolfinger and Rosenstone (1980, 30–34), for example, found no difference in farm versus urban turnout in the United States. Indeed, turnout among farmers (not all of those who live on farms are farmers) was substantially higher than any other occupational

ate cultural and demographic environment to promote high levels of voting. The fact that voting in the United States is instead far lower than in any other industrial democracy is a function, Powell finds, of the structural constraints imposed by the registration system and related election laws (such as noncompulsory voting, Tuesday instead of Sunday elections, and the like). Our interest in this chapter is in comparing the key demographic and cultural environmental factors in Central America with those in the United States and other industrial democracies. We will not explore here the institutional constraints on voting in any direct way but will look at registration and its constraints.

Powell examines three sets of factors: (1) attitudes facilitating voter turnout, (2) participation in other forms of political activity, and (3) demographic characteristics facilitating participation. Fortunately, the Central American data set included variables in each of these areas. The basic data are summarized in table 7.2. The notes to the table clarify differences between the Central American data and the comparative results for the other cases.

A strong sense of political efficacy has been found to be conducive to higher turnout. In the United States, efficacy levels are very high, with 59 percent of the population reporting that they felt politically efficacious. The seven industrial democracies have a lower level, with an average of only one-third of the respondents exhibiting an efficacious response. In Central America, with the notable exception of Panama, efficacy levels are more like those found in Europe than in the United States. With the exception of Panama, whose efficacy level approaches that of the United States, the Central American cases are somewhat below the European ones, but the differences are by no means dramatic. The lowest efficacy level is found in El Salvador, with 22 percent feeling politically efficacious, but it should be noted that the European cases *averaged* 33 percent, and in some countries it was lower. In sum, most Central Americans do not express an efficacious response to this often used civic culture item, and hence one should not expect to find a boost in voting because of a strong sense of citizen efficacy. It is also the case, however, that the responses are not dramatically lower than they are among many industrial democracies. Therefore, we should also not expect depressed levels of voting owing to low levels of efficacy.

Political trust is another key area in Powell's analysis. Our measurement of political trust is different from the classical one used by the University of Michigan Survey Research Center and employed in these European cases. Prior research has shown that the trust items proved to be unreliable and partially invalid in their capturing of low levels of citizen trust in government. Instead, we used a series of items that form a Political Support-Alienation measure that has been extensively pretested in several studies (Seligson 1983;

Honduras (%)	El Salvador (%)	Nicaragua (%)	Costa Rica (%)	Panama (%)
28	22	32	30	49
36	66	73	83	53
43	8	19	24	46
42	6.9	20	24	29
67	63	34	57	81
30	30	45	48	55

which 1 represented "none" and 7 represented "a lot." The percentages reported here are the sum of the positive end of the continuum, that is, categories 5, 6, and 7.

[c]The item was identical in all countries. It read: "During the election campaigns some people try to convince others to vote for a particular party or candidate. Have you tried to convince others how to vote: frequently, once in a while, rarely, or never?" The responses are based on those who have taken this action at least on rare occasions. The Costa Rican data come from the 1987 sample described in Note a above.

[d]The item was identical in all countries. It read: "There are people who work for one of the parties or candidates during the election campaigns. Have you worked for a candidate or party in the recent or past elections?"

[e]Basic education in Central America is generally considered to be the first six years (i.e., primary school), but to retain comparability with the data set from Powell, beyond ninth grade is used for all countries.

activism and voting, since one can assume, for example, that those who take the time and effort to work for a party will themselves expend the small amount of additional energy needed to register and then vote.

Powell found that persuasion and party work were more frequent in the United States than in the average of seven industrial democracies in his study. In Central America there is a wide range of levels. Honduras exceeds slightly the high levels found in the United States on both variables, and Panama exceeds it on persuasion and is only slightly lower on party work. Costa Rica and Nicaragua form intermediate cases, lower than the United States but higher than Europe on party work and somewhat lower on persuasion. Finally, El Salvador and Guatemala exhibit very low levels on these two activities. It is not surprising that voting levels were lowest there (see figure 7.1) and highest in Honduras, where the levels were the highest. Overall, these forms of political participation do seem associated with the vote in Central

Individual-Level Explanations of Voter Turnout: A Fourteen-Nation Comparison

We now need to turn to the question of the impact of individual-level variables on voter turnout. We divide our analysis into two sections. The first centers on the impact of major demographic variables and the second on the major attitudinal variables. We again follow the format utilized by Powell in his multination comparisons.

According to numerous studies of voting behavior in the United States, education, gender, and age are the three most important individual characteristics that help predict voter turnout. It has also been shown, however, that the relationship between these variables and turnout is not necessarily linear. This is especially true in the case of age, in which a curvilinear pattern has been encountered, such that the youngest and oldest citizens vote less than those in their middle years (Wolfinger and Rosenstone 1980, 37–60). It has been argued that this pattern emerges because only in the middle years do voters develop a stake in the system; as the aging process sets in, interest in politics is lost, and limitations of physical mobility reduce turnout. Whatever the explanation, it is important to be sensitive to the possibility of nonlinear relationships.

Powell (1986, 28–30) reports the impact of individual-level explanations for the United States and eight industrial nations (Britain, West Germany, the Netherlands, Switzerland, Finland, Canada, Austria, and Italy). He uses a parsimonious technique (of dummy variable regression) that allows the reader to see quite easily the impact of each variable.[8] We follow his presentation in table 7.3. The numbers in the table show the percentage increase in voting over the baseline category. For example, looking at the column for the United States and examining the row that is labeled "sex," one finds a −6 next to "female." This means that females are 6 percent *less* likely to vote than males when the other basic variables are held constant.[9] The table also shows that for those with the highest levels of education (postsecondary education), turnout is 35 percent higher in the United States than for those with only "basic" education (i.e., fewer than seven grades completed).

Table 7.3 contains a great deal of information, but it is easily summarized. First, there is a direct association between the impact of these basic variables and the level of turnout. For those countries, such as El Salvador and Guatemala, where turnout is lower than elsewhere in the region (see figure 7.1), our ability to predict turnout is greater. At the other extreme, Costa Rica and Honduras, where some nine out of ten respondents voted, these variables make

almost all of the countries. In every country except Costa Rica and Panama, females voted slightly less than males, when education and age are held constant. But the finding is only significant in Guatemala and Nicaragua. Only in Guatemala are the differences notable, with females 14 percent less likely to vote than males. It is appropriate to stress again that these are the differences encountered after controlling for age and education. An examination of the uncontrolled data reveals the more common pattern of much higher male voting than female voting. For the sample as a whole, 66 percent of the males voted compared with 56 percent of the females. The difference is greatest in Guatemala (76 percent versus 62 percent), El Salvador (62 percent versus 51 percent), and Nicaragua (84 percent versus 75 percent) but very small in Honduras (88 percent versus 85 percent) and practically nonexistent in Costa Rica (85 percent versus 84 percent).

Fourth, age is the variable most consistently and powerfully connected to voting in Central America. Moreover, the relationship between age and turnout is similar, with certain exceptions, to that typically found in the United States. That is, voting is less frequent among those who are younger and higher among those in the middle-age cohorts. Powell's sample did not reveal the downturn in the oldest age groups normally found among U.S. samples (see Wolfinger and Rosenstone 1980, 37–60). This may be a function of the fact that in this analysis, age is controlled by education. Since older people as a group are less well educated than the young, when education is controlled, the vote does not decline among those who are older. Of course, this thesis has its limits, since among the very old, let's say those eighty and over, the problem of mobility emerges and serves to deflate voting. Powell did find some declines in voting among those sixty years of age and older in both Britain and Switzerland. In Central America the decline among the oldest voters is noticeable in each of the six countries. In Honduras and Nicaragua the drop-off is the sharpest as one moves from the fifty- to fifty-nine-year-old group to the sixty-and-over group, declining from 17 percent to 8 percent in Honduras and 14 percent to 3 percent in Nicaragua. A clear image of the impact of age on turnout and its curvilinear pattern is shown in figure 7.2, in which the entire Central American sample is shown. A somewhat more complex pattern is revealed when the same chart is redrawn with one curve for each country (figure 7.3). We deleted the oldest cohorts in some of the countries when there were fewer than five cases in the cohort; hence not all of the countries reveal the same sharp downturn in turnout among the oldest citizens. Nonetheless, the overall pattern is quite similar.

A pattern found in Central America that does differ from the United States

Figure 7.3. *Age and Vote in Central America, by Individual Country*

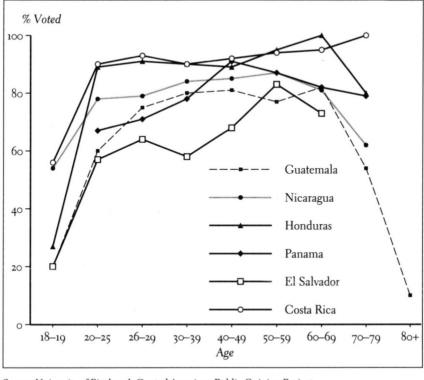

Source: University of Pittsburgh Central American Public Opinion Project.

Other Explanations for Turnout in Central America

In Powell's comparative study of turnout in industrial democracies, attitudinal variables were found, in general, to have less of an effect than the demographic variables examined above. Political efficacy, for example, was found to be a consistently significant predictor of turnout only in the United States, Britain, the Netherlands, and Italy, but in no case did it make more than a 9 percent difference in turnout. Hence, in the United States, those with high efficacy were 9 percent more likely to vote than those with low efficacy, but in Italy the difference was only 4 percent. Political interest had a greater impact, as much as 32 percent in the United States and 36 percent in Canada among those with the highest levels of interest.

In one of the very few prior statistical analyses of abstentionism in Latin America, Davis and Coleman (1983) compared industrial workers in Mexico and Venezuela. In that paper they found that efficacy was a predictor of electoral participation, as was party identification. In addition, they found that

Honduras	El Salvador	Nicaragua	Costa Rica	Panama
—	—	—	—	—
9	1	-6	-4	—[b]
6	6	-4	-5	15
2	6	-5	-6	11
10	21*	3	-4	17*
—	—	—	—	—
-1	-6	-6*	0	0
—	—	—	—	—
9*	19*	7	5	15*
7	16*	11*	0	21*
3	28*	11*	2	35*
17*	42*	14*	10*	31*
8	33*	3	7	27*

tion = postsecondary. Powell used a somewhat different scheme for the United States and still other schemes for the European cases. The effort was made to make the levels as comparable as possible given the different levels of education in each country.
[b]In Panama, there were too few cases in the basic education category to constitute an effective base group. Hence, for Panama, the basic and lower groups were combined into a single category.
[c]The baseline category was 18–19 years of age, except for Nicaragua, where the voting age is 16 and hence the base category was 16–19.

out. Note, however, that we will find important differences in diffuse support levels among nonvoters when we compare registered with unregistered citizens. Specific support played a role only in Panama. In that country, abstention rates doubled, from 12.5 percent among those with the highest support for the government in power to 25 percent for those with the most negative evaluation of that government. In general, however, these attitudinal variables did not allow us to predict turnout with any great success in Central America.

Factors Predicting Registration

Thus far in this chapter we have treated all those who have abstained as if they all could have voted on election day. Clearly this is not true in all cases, since

cause of the limited number of cases of nonregistered citizens who did not vote in Panama, that country had to be excluded. Furthermore, the relatively small sample size in some of the other regression equations attenuated statistical significance. Nonetheless, the patterns, shown in table 7.5, are quite clear.

Although the small sample size makes some of the coefficients unstable and many statistically insignificant, the patterns uncovered earlier in table 7.3 are very similar to those reported now in table 7.5. Education, age, and sex have the same basic relationship to registration among nonvoters as they did to voting among the sample as a whole (i.e., registered and nonregistered voters). In Guatemala and El Salvador, where the sample sizes are largest, this pattern is clearest. More educated citizens are more likely to register even if they do not ultimately vote. In Guatemala the relationship is monotonic (i.e., registration increases for each increment in education), whereas in El Salvador only postsecondary education makes a significant increase in the probability of registration; voters with this level of education are 27 percent more likely to register than those with only a basic education. In Nicaragua and Honduras, as we found with respect to the probability of voting, education seems to make little difference.

Gender has the same impact on registration as it did on voting; controlling for education, age, and system support, females are slightly less likely to register to vote. The only difference in the trend uncovered for voting is that in Guatemala the impact of gender on registration is considerably greater. Females in Guatemala are 21 percent less likely to register, but only 14 percent less likely to vote, when education, age, and system support are controlled for.

Age operates on registration the same way it did on voting; younger voters are less likely to vote than older voters. The small sample size, however, makes these coefficients quite unstable, since we subdivide the sample into five age groups.

The most significant finding in this table is the relationship of system support to voting. This variable is the "political trust" measure used in table 7.2 but utilizes a five-item series (each item scored from 1 to 7) divided into four groups: very low, low, medium, and high. Although the results are not statistically significant, a pattern emerges that seems quite meaningful and consistent with other studies. The findings conform, for example, to the pattern uncovered by Davis and Coleman (1983) in Mexico and Venezuela.

In Honduras, and to a lesser extent in El Salvador, increased system support is related to an increased probability of registering to vote. In Honduras those with high system support are 39 percent more likely to register than those with very low system support. This conforms to our expectation that support for the political system encourages voter participation.

We at first found surprising the negative coefficients found in Nicaragua between system support and registration. The pattern was clear enough: higher system support was related to a lower probability of registration, such that those with the highest levels of system support were 21 percent *less* likely to register than those with very low system support. Upon reflection, however, we quickly realized that the dramatic change in Nicaraguan politics that occurred with the loss of the Sandinistas and the victory of the opposition party explains this finding. Those with high system support for the current system of government, that is, the one run by the incumbent party, did not support the Sandinista regime that was in power when the last election took place. Hence, those individuals who support the current system were less likely to have registered to vote during the Sandinista regime. Our system support measure is designed to measure support for the *system* of government, what David Easton (1975) called "diffuse support," and not support for the incumbent politicians (i.e., specific support). But in the Nicaraguan case, the election of 1990 brought to power a different political *system*. Hence, we can conclude that there is some evidence linking system support to voter registration in Central America, with those who support the system more likely to register than those who do not.

It proved possible to provide some additional confirmation of the reasoning we used to explain the Nicaraguan results by examining the results on two additional variables measuring support. In addition to the five-variable political support index used above, we also asked two other questions using the same scale format. One measured the degree of trust (*confianza*) the respondent had in the current government, and the second asked about the degree of trust in the armed forces. At the time of the survey, the government was controlled by the anti-Sandinista coalition, but the armed forces remained under the control of the Sandinistas. We found that for the nonvoters, support was higher for the government and lower for the armed forces among those who were not registered vote than among those who were registered to vote. Although these differences were not statistically significant ($N = 128$), the evidence reinforces the view that the failure to register during the period when the system was controlled by the Sandinistas was in part a function of the lack of trust for the government in power at that time.

Further evidence of the relationship of system support emerges from two questions that we asked the respondents. We wanted to know the reasons they had for not voting, and then we wanted to learn why they thought others had not voted. We asked these questions in each country except Costa Rica. We presented the first question (i.e., reasons for not voting) only to those who did not vote. In order to make the responses to the second question (i.e., why

nonvoting. Hence, while it is no doubt true that the reason many did not vote is because they had not registered (see the first bar in figure 7.4), this begs the question as to why they had not registered in the first place. That reason was probably expressed in response to the question as to why others did not vote. Thus the very high levels of responses in the "mistrust" of the elections category may be the best indicator of the real reasons for nonvoting.

An examination of the individual country patterns (not included in figure 7.4) is revealing. In Guatemala, for example, whereas 59 percent of the respondents said that nonregistration was the reason for their not voting, only 10 percent gave that as the reason why others did not vote. Instead, 45 percent of Guatemalans said that mistrust of the elections was the main reason for others not voting. If the "don't know" responses (26 percent of the Guatemalan total) are excluded, then mistrust as an explanation rises to 60 percent of the valid responses for Guatemala. A similar pattern emerges in El Salvador, where 62 percent of the respondents believe that mistrust of the elections is the reason why others did not vote. In Panama, mistrust is also high (41 percent), but fear of violence is higher than in any other country (26 percent). This finding is not surprising given the violence that infused all elements of the 1989 election campaign. One only need recall the vivid television images of candidate Guillermo Ford being beaten bloody to understand how much fear was involved in the decision not to vote in Panama.

We can empirically demonstrate that those who stated that others did not vote because of mistrust and fear of violence were themselves less trusting of the political system. We once again used the Political Support-Alienation five-item scale to measure the respondents' support for the political system. The scale was coded so that a low support was coded as a zero and high support as a 10.[11] The results are presented in figure 7.5. As can be seen, in every country, the respondents' own level of system support was lower among those who believed that others who did not vote did so because of mistrust of the elections than it was for those who believed that there were other reasons for not voting. Those "other reasons" included failure to register as well as personal health problems, lack of time or money to vote, and so on. In addition, in Guatemala, Honduras, and El Salvador, those who gave "fear" as an explanation for the nonvoting of others were also, on average, less supportive of the political system than those who gave "other" reasons. This pattern, which is shown in figure 7.5 for the entire sample, also holds among nonvoters.

This examination of the reasons for abstaining in Central America reveals that not all of the explanation resides in the standard socioeconomic and demographic variables examined earlier in the chapter. In Central America the credibility of the election process itself is very much in question. Those

we also found that factors rooted in the context of the region, especially system support or the lack of it, are important variables.

Specifically, we found that despite the substantial levels of violence concomitant with the elections held in El Salvador, Guatemala, and Panama, the levels of abstention were equal to or lower than those of the industrial democracies. More specifically, allowing for country variations, our data indicate that the profile of Central American electorates resembles those of Europe and the United States in terms of education, sex, age, political trust, and political efficacy. In countries with lower turnout (El Salvador and Guatemala), the data analysis showed that individual-level variables were more effective predictors of voter turnout. On the other hand, in cases in which turnout was higher (Costa Rica, Honduras, and Nicaragua), such variables had much less impact. As far as the "life cycle" patterns of electoral participation are concerned, we found a familiar inverted-U curve of participation, with both younger and older voters less likely to vote, although we did detect some evidence of higher levels of voting among first-time voters in some countries. However, on the whole, our analysis shows that neither demographic nor attitudinal variables predict much of the variance in voter turnout in Central America, a situation similar to that found in the United States and Europe. This turned our attention to another possible variable in explaining turnout: voter registration.

In comparing the registered with the nonregistered population, we found that demographic and sociocultural variables had the same impact on registration as they had on voting. One interesting finding, however, is that system support is correlated with registration. That is, we found that the higher the level of system support, the greater the probability of registration among nonvoters. Hence, we conclude that maintaining high turnout in the future will depend on the political systems of Central America being able to establish and maintain their legitimacy. The lesson of Mexico in this regard is an important one for Central American leaders. In Mexico, where many voters have become frustrated with years of one-party rule and electoral manipulation by the PRI, voter turnout has fallen so low that it has worried many PRI leaders. In the 1980s many academics were severely critical of the elections taking place in Central America. They were criticized as being merely "demonstration elections," fostered by the United States to justify continued aid to counterinsurgency policies. There is something to be said for that argument, but perhaps in spite of the questionable etiology of these elections in Central America, they are becoming a routine feature of the political landscape. If political leadership is seen to rotate because of such elections, some degree of system support may be generated, which may sustain voter registration levels

7. The turnout rates for the non–Central American cases is taken from Powell (1986, 38). These data are for the eligible (i.e., voting-age) population. The Central American data are from the six surveys. Since the survey was conducted among voting-age adults in each country, all of the respondents were eligible, although not all were registered voters, as will be discussed below. We had to adjust the figures reported here to take account of those respondents who were too young to vote in the election prior to the survey.

8. Powell demonstrates that this technique produces nearly identical results to Logit, the technique normally applied to dichotomous dependent variables.

9. Powell uses, as we do, education, sex, and age. He also uses party identification (as measured by the response to a question regarding "feeling close to" a political party). Since we did not include that item in our Central America surveys, we do not report it or control for it in our results. Powell finds that party identification produces an 18 percent increase in turnout in the United States and an average of 17 percent in the other eight industrial democracies in his study. The impact of party identification is greatest in the Netherlands (33 percent) and least in Italy (3 percent). In every country it is significant.

10. For a discussion of voting qualifications in Costa Rica, see Seligson (1987).

11. The five items each ranged from 1 to 7. These were summed and yielded a range of 5 to 35. To convert this to a scale of 0 to 10, 5 points were subtracted from each total, and the total was then divided by 3.

References

Booth, John A., and Mitchell A. Seligson, eds. 1989. *Elections and Democracy in Central America*. Chapel Hill: University of North Carolina Press.

Córdova Macías, Ricardo. 1989. "El Salvador: Análisis de las elecciones presidenciales de marzo de 1989." *Presencia* (San Salvador) (April–June): 87–103.

——. 1992. "Partidos y elecciones en El Salvador (1982–1989)." *Revista de ciencias sociales* (Universidad de Costa Rica) (December 1991–March 1992): 147–72.

Davis, Charles L., and Kenneth M. Coleman. 1983. "Who Abstains? The Situational Meaning of Nonvoting." *Social Science Quarterly* 64 (December): 764–76.

Easton, David. 1975. "A Re-assessment of the Concept of Political Support." *British Journal of Political Science* 5 (October): 435–57.

Gandásegui H., Marco. 1990. "Democracia, intervención y elecciones: Panamá, 1989." *Revista mexicana de sociología* 52 (October–December): 371–89.

Hernández R., Oscar. 1991. "Análisis del abstencionismo en las elecciones presidenciales de Costa Rica en el período 1953–1986." *Anuario de estudios centroamericanos* 16 and 17: 117–37.

Instituto Histórico de Centroamérica (IHCA). 1991. "Como votó Nicaragua: Los resultados electorales." *ENVIO* (Managua) (April): 1–24.

Katosh, John P., and Michael W. Traugott. 1981. "Consequences of Validates and Self-Reported Voting Measures." *Public Opinion Quarterly* 45, no. 4:519–35.

Latin American Studies Association (LASA). 1984. "The Electoral Process in Nicaragua: Domestic and International Influences." Report of the Latin American Studies Association Delegation to Observe the Nicaraguan Election. Austin, Tex., November 19.

——. 1990. "Electoral Democracy under International Pressure." Report of the Latin American Studies Association Commission to Observe the 1990 Nicaraguan Election. Pittsburgh, March 15.

Molina Chocano, Guillermo. 1990. "Honduras: Crisis, economía, elecciones y sistema político (1980–1990)." *Revista mexicana de sociología* 52 (October–December): 301–14.

Muller, Edward N., Thomas O. Jukam, and Mitchell A. Seligson. 1982. "Diffuse Political Support and Antisystem Political Behavior: A Comparative Analysis." *American Journal of Political Science* 26 (May): 240–64.

THE IMPACT OF
ELECTION OBSERVERS
IN CENTRAL AMERICA

Margaret E. Scranton

This chapter analyzes external observers at national elections in Panama in 1984, 1989, and 1994. Because of differences in these elections, and concomitantly in the roles observers played in each one, Panama's experience provides a good case for enhancing our understanding of the impact of external observers. In 1984 observers exerted little influence on the electoral process or outcome of a low-visibility election that was tightly managed by the military regime.[1] The United States was harshly criticized for certifying as fair results that were not only extraordinarily close but also vehemently challenged by the opposition. The 1989 election was also managed by the military, but this context was characterized by high visibility and priority status in U.S. foreign policy. Observers played a critical role in 1989, exposing fraud and attempting to mediate before the government annulled the election.[2] In 1994 Panama's first post–U.S. invasion, postmilitary election drew little attention from the press or U.S. officials. An independent, nonpartisan Electoral Tribunal supported by domestic verification transcended the role external observers played as guarantors of the electoral process. External observers accurately verified that domestic actors behaved exactly as they should, but their impact was incidental; internal developments in Panama accounted for the adherence to the law and democratic norms. The Panamanian case thus provides three different electoral experiences, within one national context and two regime types, in which our expectations about external observers can be assessed.

Sources consulted in this research included personal interviews with candidates, government officials, and nonpartisan actors; personal observation of the 1994 election; and primary documentation cited in the list of references.[3]

and availability of information to citizens; (e) openness and fairness of the registration process during the preelection period and ease of registration and verification procedures; and (f) presence of foreign and domestic political pressures that elevate the stakes of the election.

2. Assess the electoral process: (a) operation of identification procedures on election day, particularly whether citizens are allowed to vote without appearing on the official registry or having proper identification; (b) availability of ballots, hours and conditions of operation, secrecy and security of ballots; (c) transparency of the scrutiny of ballots, tabulation procedures, and duplication of tally sheets for various authorities; (d) transmittal of local and regional results to counting centers; (e) transparency of national tabulation and disclosure of results; and (f) provision of due process for claims of electoral violations.

3. Assess appropriate implementation of electoral outcomes: (a) the scheduled installation of successful candidates, or (b) the scheduled implementation of provisions enacted through referenda.

The trend has been for all three phases to be monitored, especially by OAS delegations, although many missions still confine themselves to election day activities. According to William Crotty, a political scientist who observed seven elections in six countries, the election day phase remains the most commonly used indicator for judging fairness. Echoing John Booth's comprehensive definition of participation, Crotty finds this unfortunate because although "the vote certification process is important . . . it is but one part of a larger picture and taken out of context is meaningless" (Crotty 1991, 65). Elections worldwide have demonstrated that biases, restrictions, and violations during the first and last phases of the process can invalidate an apparently clean performance on election day.

Informative Functions

Electoral functions refer to what observers observe; informative functions refer to what observers report, to whom, and with what play in the media. Many observer groups hold press conferences to publicize their assessments; some also print reports. Individuals, particularly scholars and journalists, may also write about their observations. In terms of informing people and governments at home and abroad about violations, the most important of these communications channels is the press conference. When fraud is alleged, timely publicity may facilitate resolution of an electoral crisis.

sador William P. Jorden and former Colombian president Alfonso López Michelsen. At the same time, opposition parties charged that the government planned to steal the election; they invited their own observers to document expected violations. In late April a U.S. congressional delegation led by Senators Bennett Johnston and Lawton Chiles visited Panama City, met with opposition leaders, and expressed strong support for free elections (U.S. Dept. of State 1984b). None of the external observers were present during the pre-election stage of the campaign or for the drafting and approval of the new electoral code. None stayed for an extended period, including the ten-day counting period.

The Electoral Context

The defining issue in 1984 was the future of the military. This, plus the fact that Dr. Arnulfo Arias had moved against the senior officer corps before, raised the PDF's stakes. On May 1, five days prior to the election, military leaders sent a letter to Dr. Arias warning him against "attempts to affect the structure of the institution" (Kinzer 1984a, 5). His opponent, Dr. Barletta, pointed out the obvious implication, saying "the temptation [would] be open to have another coup" (Kinzer 1984a, 5).

Electoral Functions

Party representatives interviewed on election day by Stephen Kinzer reported no major problems. Raúl Arias de Para, a Christian Democrat who wrote a detailed analysis of the election, reported that copies of fraudulent identification documents were shown to international observers from the United States (Ambassador Jorden) and Colombia (former president Michelsen) on election day but neither took any action (1984, 75). Arias de Para also reported that two U.S. observers (Gastil and Vaughn) were among many who testified about paramilitary violence against voters before an official poll supervisor; no arrests resulted (1984, 110–11). Ambassador Jorden, who observed the balloting in the interior, characterized the election as "a demonstration of democracy and a magnificent political process" (Kinzer 1984c, A11). As the polls closed, after some delays but as yet no serious violations, Luis Martínez, Arias's spokesman, commented, "There have been plenty of irregularities, but nothing earth-shaking" (Kinzer 1984b, A13). The next day, May 7, as votes were slowly being counted, international observers were reported as having "seen no major problems" (Kinzer 1984c, A11).

Nonetheless, between May 6 and 10, results from 2,124 *mesas* (out of a total

The report by Vaughn, Drinan, and Gastil discussed numerous procedural violations and raised the question of whether the apparent fraud during the counting process was sufficient to merit a condemnation of the election (U.S. Dept. of State 1984a, app. G). Neither this report nor any comments by delegation members, attributed or leaked on a background basis, appeared in the U.S. press or congressional documents. An extract from the report was printed in Panama's *La Prensa* on June 1, 1984. Against the delegation's objective of accurately documenting imperfections in the procedure, the confidential report also stressed the objective of supporting Panama's democratic transition and the risks that an electoral crisis or another coup would pose. The authors questioned whether the flaws in the election were sufficiently egregious to merit U.S. condemnation. They urged the administration to facilitate a meeting of the protagonists to devise a solution. They recommended, on balance, that the prospects for continued democratization were better under Barletta, despite questions that could be raised about the election. The most serious note of caution sounded by the report concerned the influence of the PDF and the need for the United States to support the development of civil institutions.

Finally, after Washington declined to challenge the stalled counting process, the U.S. Embassy made the following confidential assessment of the significance of the 1984 election:

> It had been hoped that successful national elections would resolve the leadership crisis in which Panama has been mired since the untimely death of General Omar Torrijos in 1981, and provide the new government a legitimacy that, it can be argued, has been absent since the coup of 1968. It had been hoped that improved leadership and legitimacy would cure the sense of drift that has plagued Panama, and increase the country's national self-confidence. It had further been hoped that a successful election would heal old wounds in the body politic, improve Panama's image abroad and eventually the investment climate, and permit leaders to devote more time and attention to national problems rather than political maneuvering. At best, however, Barletta will have squeaked out a narrow win, probably by less than 10,000 votes. At worst, his election may be seen as seriously tainted both at home and abroad. (U.S. Dept. of State 1984d)

The straightforward and relatively accurate assessments made in this cable, the confidential observers' report, and Cason's analysis differed significantly from the administration's public pronouncements, which emphasized the fact that the first direct presidential election in sixteen years was held as

Observers and Their Capacities

Since so many domestic and foreign actors affected this election, separate influences are difficult to disentangle. Many more international observers, including more regional delegations, participated in 1989. In addition, some external observers, notably former president Jimmy Carter, assumed multiple missions: independent observer, activist prodding the electoral process forward, and mediator.

As in 1984, the official process of inviting and credentializing international observers was fitful and uncertain. Attempting to control who observed, the government ordered that U.S. citizen observers must obtain visas, which were only available from its consulate in Tampa; other nations' delegations also encountered entry problems. Then, the government applied pressure directly on hotels in Panama, requiring them to obtain permission from the Ministry of Commerce before registering observer guests and prohibiting private meetings on hotel premises (NRIIA/NDI 1989, 10). Finally, the government limited the number of visas issued to various delegations; the NDI/NRIIA delegation, for example, was issued only twenty official visas.

Nonetheless, oppositionists in Panama and external observers were determined to scrutinize the election; their dogged efforts, along with international press attention and the prevailing regional norm of accepting observers (particularly the Carter Center, the Center for Democracy, and NDI/NRIIA), secured entry for most of the invitees. A local group, Support Commission for International Observers, assisted with lodging, travel, and other material and logistic support (Comité de Apoyo 1989). One of its leaders went so far as carrying suitcases of cash to pay hotel and other bills for the roughly four hundred delegates under his care.

Among the observers present in 1989 were some with ample experience in the region and elsewhere. Delegates from the NDI had been working with opposition parties and other groups in Panama since 1987, training local personnel for poll-watching and parallel vote-counting operations.

Electoral Functions

The Council of Freely Elected Heads of Government sent a fact-finding mission, organized and funded by the NDI, to Panama on March 12–16, 1989, to survey election laws and procedures and prepare a detailed background report (NRIIA/NDI 1989, 8).[5] An eight-member NDI/NRIIA advance team also visited Panama during the preelection period (April 3–10) to facilitate the entry, access, and operations of observer missions. As a result, U.S.-sponsored delegations were extremely well briefed.

These and other announcements had an immediate impact throughout the region. Several Latin American governments, notably Venezuela, Peru, Brazil, and El Salvador, also condemned the Panamanian government or pronounced the opposition victorious. These reactions were, however, tempered with cautions against U.S. intervention. A similar tension between a willingness to condemn the Panamanian government and wariness of U.S. intervention also characterized the OAS's May 17 session on the election.

Later, both the NDI/NRIIA delegation and the Panamanian Support Committee published detailed reports documenting their findings along with official statements, legal documents, and electoral data. The Support Committee's publication included a joint communiqué approved by 279 observers from twenty-one countries, reports from nine observer groups, and numerous personal testimonies denouncing fraud and human rights violations. The NDI/NRIIA publication also included communiqués issued by the Panamanian Episcopal Conference on April 5 and May 11, 1989.

These reports and documents made a broadly persuasive case supporting allegations of fraud and human rights violations. Issued at different times, and using various sets of results and making various assumptions about valid and invalid votes and various projections, these reports concluded that the Democratic Alliance of Civic Opposition (Alianza Democrática de Oposición Civilista—ADOC) won between 67 and 75 percent of the vote. Unlike 1984, when most observers judged the election to be close and differed over which side held a vote margin of two thousand to four thousand, in 1989 the opposition victory was overwhelming. Some observers even reported that *mesas* with heavy PDF voting were giving ADOC a majority.

Even more significant, in shaping U.S. policy and public opinion, were graphic images of paramilitary repression of protesters and candidates on May 10, images that were transmitted on CNN and nightly network news programs and subsequently on the covers of news magazines. These pictures, particularly the one of candidate Billy Ford wearing a white shirt splattered with blood, solidified a judgment in U.S. policy and public opinion that ADOC was the rightful victor. These pictures, and the demonstration that provided the setting for them, were the indirect result of the press coverage and the presence of international observers. It is impossible to assess the degree to which observers contributed to the opposition's conviction that their victory was being stolen and the determination of leaders and followers to demonstrate. Opposition leaders perceived an opportunity to make their case to international audiences and made a courageous effort to do so.

At this point, the situation in Panama escalated to priority status in U.S. foreign policy, and the input of external observers was overshadowed by

Conducted under a civilian regime, the campaign had all the features of modern democratic politics: public opinion polls, candidate debates, radio and television commercials, newspaper and leaflet advertisements, car caravans, rallies, and ubiquitous banners, T-shirts, and baseball caps. All these activities were conducted in an atmosphere of comparative moderation and tolerance. Most journalists and observers compared the campaign and election day to a fiesta.

Behind the appearance of normalcy were solid and important steps toward institutionalizing democratic norms and practices. Work by the Catholic Church and the Commission of Justice and Peace brought the parties to the point of signing a document, the Compromise of Santa María Antigua, in which they pledged to respect and abide by stated rules of the game. Similarly, an initiative by the United Nations Development Program to assist the parties in articulating a consensus on national needs stimulated an unprecedented dialogue among leaders that encompassed former friends and enemies and new political voices.

Instead of fraud, the dominant topic of debate among journalists, analysts, and observers was which candidate would place second, since the PRD alliance was maintaining a clear lead for first place. At visits to candidates' headquarters and the Electoral Tribunal, observers were most interested in ballot format, contingency plans for delivering tallies to counting centers, parties' platforms and supporters, and women candidates.

Observers and Their Capacities

The 1994 election attracted the largest number of observers, with more than two thousand national and international observers credentialed by the Electoral Tribunal. External observers included delegations from Carter's Council of Freely Elected Heads of Government/Carter Center, the OAS, CAPEL, the Episcopal Church, and numerous governments. Notable individuals present on election day included Carter, former Colombian president Belisario Betancur, Salvadoran monsignor Oscar Rivera y Damas, former president of Belize George Price, former Costa Rican president Rodrigo Carazo, and former ambassador Vaughn.[6] Most had experience observing elsewhere and participated in an extensive program of briefings in Panama.

Electoral Functions

Most external observers arrived during the week preceding the Sunday, May 8 election, and most departed by Monday, matching the expectation that elec-

toral settings. These experiences suggest some tentative generalizations that may be tested with data from other countries and elections.

Expectations about the electoral context, particularly the stage in the democratization process during which an election is held, gained the most support and gave the most insight about observers' functions and impact. Both the nature of missions and observers' abilities to carry out electoral and informative functions were contingent on regime choices; these choices were the predicted ones for the stages in Panama's democratic transition.

Also differentiating the ability of U.S. observers, in 1984 compared with 1989, to assess events fully and accurately was the international context in which their findings were made. Former ambassadors Vaughn and Jorden were as well versed in Panamanian affairs and knowledgeable about the participants as were the members, and particularly the advisers, to the 1989 NDI/NRIIA delegation. However, in 1984, findings that suggested an ambiguous or fraudulent electoral outcome fit neither prevailing expectations in Washington nor the needs of U.S. policy toward Panama or the region. In contrast, in 1989, U.S. policy was rhetorically, financially, organizationally, and perceptually geared toward delegitimizing Noriega's government. This political difference accounted for not only more U.S. observers in 1989, supplied with more financial resources, but also a policy context ready and eager to receive their findings. In 1989 external observers brought "good news," which the administration eagerly promoted. In 1994 the United States was neutral toward candidates and fully committed to a transparent process; observers brought good news, but Panama was such a low priority that the exemplary election was barely noticed.

Concomitantly, the role of the media—an important aspect of the political context—was also different in 1984 and 1994 compared with 1989. The Panamanian election was more salient in 1989, since Noriega had by then been indicted in U.S. federal court and publicized as a narco-dictator; this yielded more coverage than in 1984. Thus, violence and repression by the Panamanian government, which occurred in the aftermath of both elections, became a salient issue in 1989, after being ignored in 1984.

The depth of citizen participation also differed across elections, largely as a direct result of the opposition's conviction in 1989 that the previous election had been stolen at the counting stage. Thousands of citizens were trained as poll watchers for 1989; since their training was far better than was provided in 1984, their performance was more effective in 1989. Similarly, the Catholic laity's quick count procedure involved hundreds of volunteers and local priests. In 1994 the breadth of participation was even wider, with the addition of a new set of roles, volunteer electoral delegates, and functionaries, supple-

pendent electoral organization, were the crucial factor in impeding fraud on and after election day (Garber 1989, 71).

One lesson that was learned effectively in Panama (as it had been elsewhere) was that the government was most likely to attempt to influence the outcome at the counting stage. Analysts frequently cited the aphorism attributed to Panamanian jurist José Dolores Moscote: "El que escruta, elige" (He who counts, elects). Past instances of fraud at the counting stage account for the emphasis between the elections, among oppositionists in Panama and among government and private organizations throughout the hemisphere, in developing procedures and training personnel to perform parallel counts and to conduct quick counts on a reliably sampled basis. Clearly, the ability of an opposition to produce its own tallies and projections, along with verification and endorsement by external observers, was a decisive asset for the opposition in 1989. However, mastering techniques to monitor and challenge the counting process was not the most important issue for 1994. The church was so confident in the Electoral Tribunal that it said that the results of its parallel count would remain secret and only be made public in the event of serious discrepancies.

Instead of the counting process, future election reforms may be addressed to the activity mentioned in the second, less frequently discussed part of Moscote's admonition: "El que escruta, elige. Pero él que nombra, influye, gobierna y manda" (He who counts, elects. But he who nominates, influences, governs and commands). The more transparent the election process becomes, the more important will be the choices made before and during the campaign. If Moscote's insight is correct, future political power struggles will center on the nomination of candidates and construction of coalitions.

Notes

1. Relatively little has been published about the 1984 election, which has been characterized by academics, journalists, and many Panamanians as being stolen by the military. Former president Barletta has consistently denied charges of fraud. Judging the accuracy of those accusations is beyond the scope of this chapter, although the author takes the position that the election was quite close and hotly contested by both sides. This chapter presents previously unpublished findings, based on Panamanian and U.S. sources, particularly the findings of a U.S. observer delegation.

2. Since these events have received considerable press coverage and analytical treatment, the author presents a condensed treatment of the 1989 election. Readers seeking additional details should consult Scranton (1991), (Koster and Sánchez 1990), Dinges (1990), and Kempe (1990).

national Affairs (NRIIA/NDI). 1989. *The May 7, 1989 Panamanian Elections*. Washington, D.C.: NDI/NRIIA.

Panamá. Contraloría General de la República. 1991. *Panamá en cifras: Años 1980–1990*. November.

" 'Proceso electoral fue todo un exito': Valdez." 1994. *La Prensa*, May 9, 4.

Rouquie, Alain. 1986. "Demilitarization and the Institutionalization of Military-Dominated Polities in Latin America." In *Armies and Politics in Latin America*, rev. ed., edited by Abraham F. Lowenthal and J. Samuel Fitch, 444–77. New York: Holmes and Meier.

Scranton, Margaret E. 1991. *The Noriega Years: U.S.-Panamanian Relations, 1981–1990*. Boulder, Colo.: Lynne Rienner.

——. 1992. "Panama's Democratic Transition." *Midsouth Political Science Journal* 13 (Spring): 107–28.

Swaney, David. 1991. "OEA: Una carta de brokopondo." *Americas* 43:1, 57.

"Transcript of Session on the Vote in Panama." 1989. *New York Times*, May 10, 6.

United States Department of State. 1984a. Confidential Airgram 002005. "The 1984 Panamanian Election: The Question of Fraud and Voting Irregularities." September 20.

——. 1984b. Confidential Panama 04433. "CODEL Johnston Discusses Elections and Post-electoral Period with Opposition Candidates." April 24.

——. 1984c. Confidential Panama 04684. "Panamanian Elections—The Question of Fraud." April 30.

——. 1984d. Confidential Panama 05238. "Panamanian Elections—Looking Ahead." May 12.

——. 1984e. Panama 03827. "President Illueca to Invite Senator Kennedy and Five Others to Observe Panamanian Elections." April 10.

——. 1984f. Panama 04191. "Panamanian Elections: Voting Procedures and Electoral Safeguards." April 18.

"UN Pursues Peace Process in Central America." 1989. *UN Chronicle* (December): 15–17.

Weisberg, Jacob. 1990. "Guatemala Diarist: Poll Hacks." *New Republic*, December 10, 47.

politics. Between us we have served as official, invited observers representing three different institutions in three Central American elections—including both the Nicaraguan elections of 1984 and 1990.[2] Rather than the quality of the Nicaraguan elections, our concern is with election observation itself, its functions, impacts, and limitations.

International election observation inevitably carries with it political significance. Observers do not serve merely as windows onto an election process, for, as the Heisenberg principle asserts, observers affect the observed, even when they attempt to remove themselves from any involvement in the process observed. The impact of international observers is more acute. In instances such as the 1984 and 1990 Nicaraguan elections, they actively impinged on the behaviors of both elites and masses, serving as players who importantly and repeatedly altered the elections' unfolding. We view election observation has having both a practical or technical side bearing on election organization and conduct and, perhaps more important, a symbolic/political aspect. In Nicaragua and other recent Central American votes, election observation was imbued with strikingly divergent meanings across cases and actors.

Within this variation in meaning, we argue that international observation signifies a lack of regime legitimacy and political trust as well as incomplete democratization. We further suggest that the juxtaposition of conditions creating a simultaneous desire for Nicaraguan political elements and foreign entities to utilize extensive observation is exceedingly rare. Our assessment of the prospects for election observation by external actors is somewhat less optimistic than that of many commentators, but we see a real hope for internal election observation.[3]

We begin with the background for the Nicaraguan case before turning our attention to range and meaning of election monitoring in the 1984 and 1990 Nicaraguan elections.

Elections in the Context of the Nicaraguan Revolution

The Sandinista National Liberation Front (Frente Sandinista de Liberación Nacional—FSLN) led a coalition of opponents that toppled the Somoza dynasty in 1979. The new government acted to undermine the economic base of the Somoza regime and its allies and to implement significant social, economic, and political reforms that included improved human rights performance, establishment of a mixed economy by greatly expanding government ownership in key economic sectors, and policies of redistribution of services and income to benefit the working classes. It also sought to broaden the FSLN's

In this period, the Central American heads of state successfully negotiated the Central American Peace Accord. Under its terms Nicaragua moved rapidly toward negotiating a settlement with the contras, effectively recognizing the insurgents as a legitimate political force (LASA 1988, 26–31). This diminished military threat of the contras benefited the civic opposition within Nicaragua. It gained greater freedom in compliance with the Central American Peace Accord and subsequent agreements (LASA 1990, 10). In anticipation of the scheduled 1990 election, opposition activity within Nicaragua grew rapidly, encouraged enthusiastically by the United States. Ongoing production declines and hyperinflation had induced the government to abandon much of its socialist/populist economic program and adopt draconian liberalization measures in 1988 and 1989. These actions deepened popular discontent.

The 1990 Election

As U.S. hostility and domestic opposition grew and other Western assistance declined in the late 1980s, the revolutionary government turned once again to an election as a possible adaptive mechanism. At the Central American presidential summit of early 1989, the Sandinista government agreed to move the 1990 elections ahead ten months, to February, and with the other parties reform Nicaragua's electoral law. By August 1989 an interparty accord was reached on electoral reforms, opposition access to the media for campaigning, and a call by all parties for the contras to demobilize by the end of the year. Under heavy U.S. pressure to present a unified electoral front, fourteen quite disparate parties quickly forged the United Nicaraguan Opposition (Unión Nicaragüense Opositora—UNO) and selected Violeta Barrios de Chamorro as its nominee for president.[6] Although eight other microparties ran presidential and legislative candidates, only UNO and the FSLN were significant contenders.

The Nicaraguan government again invited and even promoted international observation of the election, but this time at a level never before attempted anywhere. The United Nations and Organization of American States (OAS) mounted the most elaborate and formal observation efforts; the Council of Freely Elected Heads of Government (the Carter Commission) also made a major and sustained effort. The United Nations and OAS had large permanent staffs, supplied with vehicles and sophisticated communications equipment; the Carter Commission maintained a small permanent staff. On election day itself, the United Nations had some 240 observers, the OAS 450. Other groups with extensive involvement included Hemisphere Initiatives (HI), a private liberal-leaning organization based in Boston, and the Latin American Studies Association (LASA), a scholarly association. Each sent small observer

Local poll watchers and supervisory bodies representing various political parties and citizens' groups should conduct an extensive, intensive, and systematic scrutiny of all aspects of the electoral process.

International observers play generally limited but sometimes crucial roles. Except in small countries, external monitors are unlikely to have the numbers or resources to match even a modest local monitoring effort. External observers, however, can supplement and validate local observation mechanisms and findings, facilitate the electoral process, and interpret the election to the international community. In highly polarized polities, the presence of external observers may also create or enlarge the political space that facilitates and protects domestic monitors, making their work easier.

Nicaragua's 1984 and 1990 elections incorporated an extensive and successful system of internal monitoring, along with international observation. Nicaraguans, through the Supreme Electoral Council (CSE), the Council of Political Parties, and party poll watchers, participated at every level over the full electoral process, from registration through ballot counting. External observers in 1984 concentrated mainly on the electoral rules and their implementation and on election day, whereas in 1990 they assessed the fairness of the entire election process, playing more extensive, intensive, and systematic roles than in 1984.

The unprecedented scope of the Nicaraguan 1990 external monitoring effort arose from the set of historical conditions just discussed. A confluence of domestic and foreign pressures produced an unusual conjunctural moment, one in which an independent country for the first time invited international observation of its electoral process from the initial preelection rule making through the inauguration of the new government.

The United Nations' effort in Nicaragua in 1990 exemplifies the potential sweep of observer groups' activities. It implemented a three-phased operation. Beginning in August 1989 a small U.N. staff evaluated voter registration efforts, the organizing activities of parties and candidates, and the early application of election rules by the government. In December, at the start of the official campaign period, an expanded staff monitored media coverage and advertising and began sending teams to each of the regions of Nicaragua to observe the campaign, check on harassment, and investigate complaints. United Nations observers helped mediate the resolution of disputes at local and national levels. The agency expanded its number of personnel again in February to watch voting and ballot counting and to verify the tally through both a quick vote count and a parallel count.[7] As the election's outcome was becoming known, U.N. representative Elliot Richardson assisted the OAS's

about the electoral law. These volunteers, representing eight parties, then trained staff for more than seven hundred registration and voting places. Hemisphere Initiatives reported that it found the training session "a model of nonpartisan, democratic and civic education" (HI 1989b, 2). Here again observer groups validated Nicaragua's efforts to lay the foundation for fair elections.

Election Disputes

International election observation occurs in countries experiencing high levels of polarization and where democratic transitions of power have not become routinized. In such political environments, serious conflicts between partisans are likely. As a result, international observers are drawn more overtly into the political arena. They may become complaint investigators as well as mediators to resolve disputes. In these instances, observers act not as bystanders but as fact finders, intervenors, referees, and deterrents to conflict and manipulation, as the following situations illustrate.

Observers in Nicaragua in 1990 investigated hundreds of cases of purported intimidation of candidates and electoral officials; they also monitored the activities of the contras (Uhlig 1990, 4). In general, they found most claims of intimidation exaggerated. For example, near the conclusion of the election campaign, Elliot Richardson, head of the U.N. observer group, commented that a wide discrepancy existed between the prevalence of intimidation charges and the actual evidence (Hockstader 1990, A21). The U.N. report released in February 1990 discounted the overwhelming majority of incidents as being part of any election campaign and having nothing to do with intimidation (Stanfield 1990, 397). On the other hand, Richardson in January reported that increased attacks by the contras had "an adverse effect on the electoral process" (Sharkey 1990, 28).

Observers often moved beyond inquiry to action. In one case, Carter intervened on behalf of a Nicaraguan lawyer who represented opposition candidates and claimed to be the subject of attacks. The former president discussed the case with the vice minister of the interior and then announced that the lawyer would get police protection (Kurylo 1989a, A6). During the Nicaraguan campaign, incidents or threats of violence at campaign rallies were commonplace, and observer delegations often tried to solve or prevent such problems. In Nandaime, for example, observers intervened to convince the FSLN mayor to stop making threats about an upcoming UNO rally. One of us, along with members of a variety of delegations (OAS, the Carter Commission, Center for Democracy, National Democratic Institute, National Republican Institute, and HI) attended this rally on November 19 because these groups

paign coverage on television as well as monitored the capital's three news-papers and government and opposition radio stations. These projects included the identification of inflammatory press coverage as well as its correction (Uhlig 1990, 4).

Use of State Resources. The August 1989 political agreement establishing election rules prohibited the misuse of government resources by the FSLN in its campaign. During the campaign the government was charged with using buildings and vehicles, as well as state-owned media, inappropriately. Observ-ers investigated without coming to comprehensive conclusions. The United Nations was able to verify that the FSLN itself had paid for the use of some vehicles (interview with Horacio Boneo, February 22, 1990), but HI inferred that the FSLN had indeed misused some state resources (HI 1990a, 2).

Voting. The number of observers swelled to more than twenty-five hundred on election day (Crotty 1991, 68). Some groups of observers merely arrived on the scene, but many delegations were trained to recognize correct procedures, which included, for example, dipping each voter's thumb in an indelible dye to prevent multiple voting. With months of preparation, international ob-servers asserted before the election that they believed it would be impossible for either the FSLN or UNO to cheat without being detected.

The U.N. and OAS teams combined for the most extensive monitoring operation. Together they had almost seven hundred observers in the field on election day. With an elaborate network that deployed observers by jeep, plane, helicopter, and boat and linked them by satellite communications, they were prepared to monitor everything from military balloting to the trans-mission of vote tallies (Uhlig 1990, 4). According to the United Nations, on election day its observers visited 2,155 voting stations (*UN Chronicle* 1990a, 16). Although observer groups encountered widely scattered voting problems, they evaluated the balloting process overall as without serious flaw.

Ballot Counting. Many observers remained at polling stations to watch the votes be counted and recorded. The United Nations and OAS independently witnessed ballot counting in approximately 15 percent of all locations. They each then proceeded with their quick counts in order to be able to ascertain the validity of the results when they were reported by the CSE.

Overall, observer groups gave strong endorsements to the election process. The United Nations' postelection report is typical: "[T]he elections were conducted in a highly commendable manner, and no problems have been detected which might cast doubts on their fairness. The best evidence of this is obviously the victory of the opposition, which entertained doubts about the validity of the electoral process" (*UN Chronicle* 1990a, 16).

propriately stack the electoral deck in favor of the bourgeoisie. In contrast, non-Marxists—including the FSLN's opponents at home and abroad—have averred that no election conducted by a Marxist regime could possibly be truly free because revolutionary vanguardism and centralism could never provide a fair contest, accept defeat, or relinquish power voluntarily. Both these claims appear ludicrous in light of the role of elections in the collapse of the Eastern bloc Communist nations and in the Nicaraguan case itself. Nevertheless, such symbolic and political attributions to elections were widespread prior to 1990.

More important in this context, external election observation itself necessarily takes on symbolic and political importance to observers, to the electoral contestants, and to other actors. Thus, like holding or competing in elections, witnessing and evaluating them are acts laden with meaning and perforce are political.

The political implications of election observation are multifaceted. To observe, publicly judge, and report on the quality of an election goes beyond mere measurement. For external observers to judge the honesty or fairness of an election or to serve as a referee or mediator of conflict constitutes attributing right or wrong to institutions and processes and those participating in them. They may give or take away legitimacy from institutions or actors in the eyes of domestic and external audiences and thus differentially benefit them. To undertake election observation is, therefore, to enter directly into the internal political process of the nation holding the election and likely into its external relations as well. Election observation is thus highly likely to provoke criticism and debate about the enterprise itself and about its motives.[12] The meaning attributed to election observation by a particular actor is likely to be a function of that actor's view of what the election itself is about. The following discussion examines the significance both of the 1990 election itself and of its external observation to several sets of actors.

The 1990 Election

The Sandinistas' View. For the 1990 election the revolutionary government's goals were roughly the same as they had been in 1984: (1) to comply with constitutional requirements for a national election in 1990; (2) to win a fair election in order to bolster regime legitimacy; (3) to coopt the opponents and build an interelite consensus on the rules of the political game; and (4) to legitimize the regime externally and bring increased pressure on the United States to stop assistance to the contras and thus end the war.

The vast role for international observers in 1990 and especially the large,

UNO officials coaching an alleged voter complaining about some problem with his polling place before a Mexican television camera. When the man argued that what he wanted to say was different than the more elaborate complaint the UNO officials were coaching him to make, he was threatened with the termination of the interview and his opportunity to be on television. Campaign officials from UNO then gave the same LASA observer team a list of alleged instances of seriously fraudulent and illegal practices at several area polling places. The team took down specific details, immediately investigated each of the cases, and found that none of them was in any way true.

What was going on in these instances? Our interpretation is that UNO was compiling (manufacturing) a list of mainly bogus complaints against the CSE, the election process, and even the international observers to account for the coalition's expected defeat by the FSLN. That is, UNO was manipulating the observation process for subsequent political advantage. Later the victorious UNO leadership got in another dig at the FSLN by claiming that only the presence of international observers had prevented the planned massive fraud and permitted the UNO victory.

The United States' and the Contras' View. By 1990 the United States had shifted from trying to disrupt and discredit the Nicaraguan election, as it had in 1984 (LASA 1984), to attempting to control its outcome. Thus it shaped and financed the opposition coalition and kept the contras together in order to maintain maximum pressure on the government, polity, and economy (Robinson 1992; LASA 1990). The contras, in accord with U.S. wishes, vowed to keep fighting until they were satisfied that the election had produced an acceptable result. The U.S. government therefore viewed election observers as ambivalently as did UNO. On the one hand, the United States endorsed international observation efforts as guarantors of fairness. The Bush administration even sought to send an official U.S. observer delegation but was rebuffed by the Nicaraguan government. A delegation from the congressionally funded Center for Democracy was also denied visas, apparently for publishing distorted accounts of campaign events (LASA 1990, 29–33).[16] Ultimately the Carter Commission included among its own ranks several of the erstwhile members of the unapproved official U.S. delegation, thus partially finessing the issue of U.S. observers (LASA 1990, 32–33).

On the other hand, the United States appeared ready to make its acceptance of the outcome and of the observers' certification of fairness conditional on a result acceptable to the U.S. government (a Sandinista loss). Misled by the polls, U.S. officials expected a Sandinista victory right up until the election and began hedging about willingness to accept even an observer-approved election. Robinson reports a high-level State Department official as

out of hand by most nations. However, the Nicaraguan government and its opposition jointly invited this involvement, which, moreover, coincided with the larger, general missions of all three external entities—preserving peace, reducing violent conflict, curtailing armed external intervention in the domestic affairs of nations, and nurturing democracy. Off-the-record conversations with many diplomats and observer team members also revealed that many OAS member states' participation was animated by a desire to help remove the FSLN from power in Nicaragua by a means other than the violent, interventionist, U.S.-backed contra insurgency. Additionally, the OAS and U.N. staffs developed a further institutional interest as their observation missions unfolded: they began to view such activity as a possible expansion of the role and scope of their agencies and thus as a source of new career opportunities.

The LASA delegation, charged to report to the membership of the association, consisted of thirteen members, nine of whom had done prior work on Nicaragua or Central America. Most members thus could benefit directly in career or research terms from participating in the delegation. Several members of the delegation, but by no means all, were or had been rather sympathetic or open minded toward the goals of the Nicaraguan revolution, if not its excesses. A majority of the delegation probably desired to use the mission to help thwart an anticipated continuation of U.S. antagonism toward Nicaragua or a U.S. discrediting of the election as in 1984. The LASA report, while extensively documenting the election and noting some flaws in the procedures, was also sharply critical of U.S. intervention in the election.

Hemisphere Initiatives (HI), a nonprofit organization created to promote democracy in Central America, an end to conflicts in the region, and sound and equitable investment and development, sent its first delegation to Nicaragua in June 1989 and later followed with five more. Its delegations met with government, opposition, and interest group leaders, in Managua as well as in various regions, and with members of other observer groups, much as LASA did. Hemisphere Initiatives undertook several information creation roles. In August HI published a briefing book on Nicaragua, then later a press kit, followed by periodic updates—for example, a report on foreign financing of UNO.[20] Most distinctively, however, HI commissioned a Washington-based survey research company to undertake two preelection polls.[21] Like LASA, HI foresaw the possibility that the Bush administration would try to impeach the integrity of the election. In its efforts to provide accurate alternative information, HI contemplated countering such expected claims. By hiring a respected firm to produce nationwide polls, HI hoped to provide validation that the election process was "clean," even if the FSLN won. Further, HI through its press kits and reports tried to provide journalists and others coming to Nic-

and a need for reassurance not available from domestic sources. Observers might wish or attempt to limit their role to detection of fraud, but we have seen in the Nicaraguan case that their roles easily expand to prevention and intervention, to facilitation and mentorship, and to the manipulation of domestic politics.

Notes

1. A partial list includes national elections for president or president and national legislature in El Salvador in 1984 and 1989, Guatemala in 1985, Nicaragua in 1984 and 1990, and Panama in 1989.

2. Patricia Richard was a member of the delegation of Hemisphere Initiatives, based in Boston, and John Booth was member of the LASA delegation to the 1990 election. Each multimember team visited Nicaragua several times in the eight months prior to the election. Booth was also a member of the 1984 LASA observation delegation. There were literally dozens of other institutionally affiliated international observer teams present in Nicaragua in 1990, in addition to hundreds of members of the international press corps. Booth also observed the 1985 Guatemalan election for the Washington Office on Latin America and International Human Rights Law Group.

3. For another assessment, see, for instance, Margaret Scranton's chapter in this volume.

4. The term *moderate* here is used not to condone the levels of repression under the revolution but to note that in comparison with neighboring El Salvador and Guatemala it was very modest and judiciously applied. In Nicaragua perhaps dozens of regime opponents were killed, and others were imprisoned or lost property; civil liberties were periodically suspended, and press censorship was practiced during several periods. In contrast, in Guatemala and El Salvador regime forces murdered tens of thousands of opponents, suspected opponents, and innocents.

5. In particular, the opposition Democratic Coordinator (CD) coalition and its candidate Arturo Cruz Sequeira chose with U.S. support not to take part in the election after having campaigned unofficially for some time. Moreover, the U.S. Embassy personnel attempted to persuade other parties to withdraw from the election. These efforts sought to reduce the scope of opposition to the FSLN and thus make the opposition appear to be purely token. For details, see Robinson (1992), LASA (1984), and *The Nation* (May 10, 1984, 639).

6. The coalition included parties of highly disparate ideological leanings—far Right, social democrats, social Christians, and Communists, among others.

7. A quick vote count resembles the "key precinct analysis" U.S. television networks undertake to project the victor in an election before all results are in and tabulated. The United Nations and OAS each used stratified samples of several hundred polling places. Each organization's observers took the results from those polls and used them to estimate the results. These estimates could then be employed by observers to assess the likely accuracy of the reported official tallies. The U.N. parallel vote count used copies of the official tallies from each polling place to obtain results, which were then compared with those of the CSE.

8. Ernesto León, director of statistics and electoral computation for the CSE, described the criteria employed in designating the 4,394 polling places in an interview with HI members on November 23, 1989. Among these were a requirement that no one have to

done by a Nicaraguan firm, Itztani. The first poll was conducted between November 25 and December 3, the second between January 13 and 19 (Bischoping and Schuman 1992, 338–39).

References

Bischoping, Katherine, and Howard Schuman. 1992. "Pens and Polls in Nicaragua: An Analysis of the 1990 Preelection Surveys." *American Journal of Political Science* 36:331–50.
Booth, John A. 1985. *The End and the Beginning: The Nicaraguan Revolution*. Boulder, Colo.: Westview Press.
———. 1986. "Election amid War and Revolution: Toward Evaluating the 1984 Nicaraguan National Elections." In *Elections and Democratization in Latin America, 1980–1985*, edited by Paul W. Drake and Eduardo Silva, 37–60. La Jolla: Center for Iberian and Latin American Studies and Center for U.S.-Mexican Studies, University of California at San Diego.
Booth, John A., and Mitchell A. Seligson, eds. 1989. *Elections and Democracy in Central America*. Chapel Hill: University of North Carolina Press.
Cornelius, Wayne A. 1986. "The 1984 Nicaraguan Elections Revisited." Latin American Studies Association *Forum* 16 (Winter): 22–28.
———. 1988. "The 1984 Nicaraguan Election Observation: A Final Comment." Latin American Studies Association *Forum* 19 (Summer): 16.
Council of Freely Elected Heads of Government. 1989. *Report on Third Pre-election Trip to Nicaragua*. Atlanta: Carter Presidential Center.
Crotty, William. 1991. "The Political Scientist as Comparative Election Observer." *PS: Political Science and Politics* (March): 64–70.
Diamond, Larry, and Juan J. Linz. 1989. "Introduction: Politics, Society, and Democracy in Latin America." In *Democracy in Developing Countries: Latin America*, edited by Larry Diamond, Juan J. Linz, and Seymour Martin Lipset, 1–58. Boulder, Colo.: Lynne Rienner.
Diamond, Larry, Juan J. Linz, and Seymour Martin Lipset, eds. 1989. *Democracy in Developing Countries: Latin America*. Boulder, Colo.: Lynne Rienner.
Drake, Paul W., and Eduardo Silva, eds. 1986. *Elections and Democratization in Latin America, 1980–1985*. La Jolla: Center for Iberian and Latin American Studies and Center for U.S.-Mexican Studies, University of California at San Diego.
Fretz, Robert. 1985. "Letter to the Editor." Latin American Studies Association *Forum* 16 (Spring): 11.
Ginsberg, Benjamin, and Alan Stone. 1991. "Preface to the Second Edition." In *Do Elections Matter?*, 2d ed., edited by Benjamin Ginsberg and Alan Stone, xiii–xv. Armonk, N.Y.: M. E. Sharpe.
Goodman, Louis W., William M. LeoGrande, and Johanna Mendelson Forman, eds. 1992. *Political Parties in Central America*. Boulder, Colo.: Westview Press.
Hemisphere Initiatives (HI). 1989a. *Establishing the Ground Rules: A Report on the Nicaraguan Electoral Process*. Boston: HI.
———. 1989b. *Nicaraguan Election Update: Implementing the Ground Rules—Phase I*. Boston: HI.
———. 1990a. *Nicaraguan Elections Final Update: Prospects for a Free and Fair Election*. Boston: HI (February).
———. 1990b. *Report on Hemisphere Initiatives' First Initiative: Monitoring the Nicaraguan Elections*. Boston: HI.
———. N.d. *Nicaragua's Elections . . . A Step towards Democracy?* Boston: HI.
Herman, Edward S., and Frank Brodhead. 1984. *Demonstration Elections: U.S.-Staged Elections in the Dominican Republic, Vietnam, and El Salvador*. Boston: South End Press.
Hockstader, Lee. 1990. "Nicaraguan Campaign Seen as Relatively Free and Open." *Washington Post*, February 17, A21, A26.
Huntington, Samuel P. 1991. "Democracy's Third Wave." *Journal of Democracy* 2, no. 2:12–34.

Vanhanen, Tatu. 1991. *The Process of Democratization: A Comparative Study of 147 States, 1980–89*. Washington, D.C.: Crane Russak.

——. 1992a. Introduction to *Strategies of Democratization*, edited by Tatu Vanhanen, 1–15. Washington, D.C.: Crane Russak.

——. 1992b. "Social Constraints of Democratization." In *Strategies of Democratization*, edited by Tatu Vanhanen, 16–35. Washington, D.C.: Crane Russak.

——, ed. 1992c. *Strategies of Democratization*. Washington, D.C.: Crane Russak.

   This prodemocracy policy serves U.S. interests in Central America in three ways. First, the policy of exporting democracy provides officials with a new consensus to guide U.S. policy in the post–cold-war world. Since the dramatic victory of Violeta Barrios de Chamorro in the Nicaraguan elections, there has been strong bipartisan agreement in Washington that fostering democracy is in the U.S. interest because it promotes political stability and forestalls revolutionary change. As one longtime observer of U.S. Latin American relations pointed out, "After a generation of strenuous internal debate in the United States on various foreign policy issues and a decade of particularly bitter divisions over Latin American policy, the idea that the United States should and can export democracy is virtually unchallenged in the Washington policy-making community" (Lowenthal 1991, viii).

   Supporting democracy also provides U.S. officials with a justification for direct military intervention. For example, the invasion of Grenada was not only explained as a "rescue mission" to protect American medical students on the island, but it was also portrayed as a campaign "to restore order and democracy to Grenada" (Carothers 1991b, 105). Similarly, the United States justified its support for the Nicaraguan contras as part of a campaign to force the Sandinistas to adopt democracy. Initially, the Reagan administration claimed that the role of the contras was only to stop the flow of arms from Nicaragua to the Salvadoran rebels. But as contra operations grew, the administration shifted its rhetoric and argued that the contras were "freedom fighters," "the moral equivalent of our founding fathers," who were fighting to restore democracy in their homeland. In his May 9, 1984, address to the nation the president portrayed the contras as heroes in a global struggle against Soviet- and Cuban-backed subversion and as allies of the United States fighting Moscow's client (Moreno 1990, 124). The Bush administration also shifted gears somewhat in justifying the U.S. invasion of Panama; the conflict with General Manuel Noriega was characterized not only as part of the "drug war" but also as part of U.S. efforts to promote democracy throughout the Western Hemisphere.

   Finally, the prodemocracy policy gives the United States carte blanche to interfere in the internal affairs of the Central American countries. For example, the United States funded the principal opposition newspaper in Nicaragua, helped organize the opposition political coalition in the 1990 elections, funded its campaign, and provided observers to the election. Similarly, elections in El Salvador and Honduras were sponsored and funded by Washington. The prodemocracy policy dramatically expanded the scope of activities that U.S. officials believed to be legitimate in the pursuit of the national interests.

quently, members of the Reagan administration strongly emphasized military (as distinct from economic and social) solutions to the problems of Central America. Rather than viewing revolutionary movements as springing from domestic economic conditions and social strains, they viewed them as the product of Cuba and the Soviet subversion. The Reagan administration viewed the Sandinista government as a client of the Soviet Union that actively sought to export revolution to the rest of Central America. Specifically, Nicaragua's military aid from Cuba and the Soviet Union threatened neighboring countries, especially by exporting Soviet arms to revolutionaries in El Salvador.

The Reagan administration made the centerpieces of its Central American policy the defeat of the Communist-led insurgents in El Salvador and the removal of the left-wing Sandinista government in Nicaragua. Reagan's pressure on the Sandinistas for a Nicaraguan democratic transition was but another tool, along with the economic embargo and the contra war, in his administration's effort to overthrow the Nicaraguan regime (Vanden and Walker 1991). Similarly, democratic and human rights principles were often subordinated to the counterinsurgency struggle in El Salvador and Guatemala. Thus, the United States supported the emergence and maintenance of elected civilian governments in the region as a means to combat perceived Soviet and Cuban adventurism. Critics of Reagan's Central American policy concluded, for example, "that democracy was nothing more than a club or weapon that the United States used whenever convenient against regimes it considered hostile, in the ongoing struggle with the Soviet Union. In Central America, it was a device to counter what the United States decried as the threat of external intervention in the region" (Tulchin and Walter 1991, 111).

The Bush administration also used democracy and elections to promote U.S. interests in Central America. George Bush, taking advantage of the collapse of the Soviet Union, believed that Sandinista radicalism could be modified, if not destroyed, through political and diplomatic pressure. Immediately after assuming office, Bush indicated that the United States would no longer attempt to overthrow the Sandinistas by military means but would instead strive for a political solution to the Nicaraguan conflict. Instead of backing contra military operations inside Nicaragua, U.S. policy emphasized peaceful opposition activities inside Nicaragua in the hope of challenging Sandinista political control. The Bush administration hoped that the February 1990 Nicaraguan elections would give the United States the opportunity to eliminate the Sandinistas. However, while the Bush administration made clear that it was retreating from the military option, it refused to abandon the contras completely. Administration officials argued against dismantling the contras until after the Nicaraguan elections, saying, "If there are no contras,

near insurrection, a view that was shared by a representative group of Salvadoran intellectuals (Baloyra 1982, 85).

Given the deteriorating situation in El Salvador, it was not surprising that there was widespread relief within the State Department when a group of progressive military officers overthrew the right-wing regime of General Humberto Romero on October 15, 1979. The young officers moved to replace the old political and economic order, fearing that unless fundamental reforms were initiated, the Salvadoran military would be swept away by the same revolutionary forces that destroyed the Nicaraguan National Guard. The removal of Romero was viewed as the last opportunity to avoid civil war.

The United States reacted enthusiastically to the reformist military coup. The day after the coup, State Department spokesman Hodding Carter III gave an optimistic account of the coup, telling reporters that "the new leadership had appealed to both the left and the right to end violence, and had promised moderate and non-violent solutions to the country's problems, including social and economic reforms and free elections" (*New York Times*, October 17, 1979). The State Department concluded that the direction of the new government was "encouraging." El Salvador became a test case of the Carter administration's policy of supporting moderates while at the same time opposing both the traditional Right and the radical Left (Moreno 1990, 71).

By supporting the new regime, the Carter administration identified the United States with social and economic policies well to the left of any previously espoused by the United States in Latin America. However, anxious to avoid "another Nicaragua," the administration combined its support for reform with military assistance in order to help the government defeat the leftist guerrillas. Washington's strategy in El Salvador was designed to avoid repeating the mistake it had made in Nicaragua, where the administration moved to replace Somoza with a moderate regime only after it was too late to prevent a leftist victory. On this occasion, the Carter administration opted to support security actions against the Left and reforms that would affect the Right. To this end, U.S. officials advocated a "clean" counterinsurgency campaign aimed at averting the indiscriminate security sweeps that had characterized Salvadoran military tactics. The Carter administration also restored lethal and nonlethal military aid to the Salvadoran military in the midst of the guerrillas' January 1980 offensive. Lethal military aid had been withheld from El Salvador since 1977 on human rights ground, and nonlethal aid was suspended in December 1979 after the brutal murder of four U.S. Roman Catholic churchwomen. The Carter administration justified this policy shift by claiming that it had compelling evidence that Cuba, Vietnam, and the Soviet Union had

Similarly, U.S. security policy in Honduras was justified in terms of promoting democracy. The democratic transition in Honduras can only be understood in the context of the interaction between the interests of the Honduran armed forces and U.S. security objectives in Central America. The central goal of U.S. policy in Honduras was to establish a safe base of operations for the Nicaraguan contras' attacks against the Sandinistas.

The Honduran armed forces under General Alvarez Martínez were willing to give the contras control of large tracts of national territory in exchange for U.S. security assistance. In fact, General Alvarez played a crucial role in selling the Reagan administration on the viability of the contra project (Gutman 1988, 49–57). The Honduran military used the Nicaraguan conflict to establish a "special relationship" with the Reagan administration in exchange for a lavish share of U.S. aid to Honduras. The United States during the Reagan administration provided Honduras with more than $440 million in military assistance (Moreno 1990, 94). Meanwhile, the anticipated "shower of dollars" for economic development did not come. United States economic aid to Honduras, although slightly higher than military aid in dollar terms, was only about $500 million between 1981 and 1988, insignificant in economic terms (U.S. Embassy, Tegucigalpa 1989). The reluctance of the United States to provide higher levels of economic aid created growing frustration in Honduras (Boletín Informativo Honduras, May 1985). For example, the progovernment Honduran Confederation of Workers (Comité de Trabajoras Hondureños—CTH) complained before the Kissinger Commission, "Honduras shows signs of true friendship, and in response we only receive from the United States cool indifference toward our economic and social problems" (Tiempo, October 18, 1984).

The de facto alliance between the Reagan administration and the Honduran armed forces would have serious consequences for internal Honduran politics. Although Honduras would hold five successive elections, the "special relationship" between the Honduran armed forces and the United States tilted the balance of power within the country in favor of the military at the very movement that Honduras was making the delicate transition toward democracy. General Alvarez, as architect of this policy, achieved unrivaled political power in a country where the military had always held a privileged position. This concentration of power endangered the process of democratization begun there in 1981.

The special relationship between United States and Honduran security services that General Alvarez established caused great concern in civilian sectors. Many Hondurans worried that the relationship would jeopardize their country's traditional internal tranquillity, endanger its security, compromise

moval of General Alvarez, his successors failed to dismantle the responsible security apparatus. Instead, repressive units such as Battalion 3/16 simply lowered their profiles. International human rights groups still charged as late as 1989 that "a steady succession of human rights abuses indicated deepening political violence in Honduras and an erosion in respect for fundamental human rights" (Americas Watch 1989, 1).

The special relationship between the Honduran military and the U.S. government frustrated the efforts of civilian leaders, especially Suazo's successor, José Azcona, to remove the contras from Honduran territory. For example, when President Azcona returned to Tegucigalpa after signing the Central American Peace Accord, which called on Honduras to dismantle contra bases in 1987, he faced the displeasure of both the U.S. Embassy and the Honduran military. Facing a cutoff of U.S. aid, Azcona bowed to the pressure and adopted a quiet policy of stalling the implementation of the peace plan.

Honduras would also fail to comply with the Tela agreement, a subsequent Central American presidential summit to refine the Central American Peace Plan. At Tela, Azcona agreed to the demobilization, repatriation, or relocation of the Nicaraguan resistance from Honduran territory. The demobilization of the contras was to have been completed within ninety days, by December 9, 1989. But the Honduran government again faced considerable pressure from the United States and its own military and was unable to comply with the Tela commitments. Azcona was so frustrated by the bullying of the Bush administration and by U.S. interference in the Honduran elections that he refused to accept the credentials of the new U.S. ambassador. However, Honduras did not dismantle the contra bases in its territory until after the Nicaraguan election, and only then after the United States supported the plan.

The Nicaraguan Election

The Nicaraguan election of 1990 also illustrates how Washington's prodemocracy policy was subordinate to U.S. security and economic interests. Promotion of democracy in Nicaragua was seen by the Bush administration as a convenient instrument for the destabilization of the Nicaraguan regime. Although George Bush shared the same general political ideology as his former boss, he entered the White House recognizing the necessity to develop a new Central American policy. The new administration recognized that Reagan's strategy of using military pressure to oust the Sandinistas had clearly failed. Instead, the new administration vigorously pursued a policy of increasing diplomatic and political pressure on the Nicaraguan government to democra-

peace plan as a mechanism for pressuring the Sandinistas. The key to the success of this strategy was to force the Nicaraguans to devise a system in which power would be contested. The administration enlisted the aid of both the Nicaraguan opposition and the Central American peace process in pressuring the Sandinistas to reform Nicaragua's election laws. Ortega had agreed at the Central American presidential summit at Costa del Sol, El Salvador, to call general and free elections no later than February 25, 1990, in effect moving the elections ahead several months. He promised to amend the electoral law, and the law relating to the mass media, to assure that all political parties would have equal access to the media. The Nicaraguan president also invited international observers, in particular the United Nations and the Organization of American States, to be present in all electoral districts in order to verify that the election process was fair at every stage.

But the Sandinistas had difficulties implementing the agreement, and the regime found itself vulnerable to both domestic and U.S. pressure. In the weeks following the Costa del Sol summit, the Sandinistas held two rounds of negotiations with opposition parties on the new election laws. These discussions quickly broke down. The Sandinistas reformed Nicaragua's election laws on April 21, despite the objections of most of the opposition parties.

A week after the passage of the election laws, fourteen opposition parties demanded further negotiations, claiming that their proposals had not been seriously considered. Some parties even threatened to boycott the upcoming election unless the government engaged in a national dialogue to agree on the rules of the game for fair and free elections. The principal bone of contention between the fourteen parties (later to become the United Nicaraguan Opposition [Unión Nicaragüense Opositora—UNO] coalition) and the Sandinista regime was the demand that parties and candidates be permitted to receive political contributions from foreign sources. Because the Sandinistas controlled the entire resources of the Nicaraguan state, the opposition claimed that it would need foreign assistance in order to compete in truly fair elections (HI 1989a, 4).

The Bush administration backed the Nicaraguan opposition by making it clear that the United States would not accept the legitimacy of the election unless further reforms were made in the election laws. The president described the newly passed reforms in harsh terms: "[R]estrictive new election and press laws have been pushed through the Sandinista controlled legislature. These laws have been unilaterally imposed, and the proposals of the Nicaraguan opposition parties have been ignored. The result is a stacked deck against the opposition and stacked rules of the game" (Bush 1989).

Ortega, facing the specter of an opposition boycott of the 1990 elections and

abuses during the Reagan administration, the endowment's charter had been amended in 1985 to bar direct aid to candidates for office.

In more direct U.S. involvement, the U.S. Embassy in Managua used its financial and persuasive powers to help unify fourteen anti-Sandinista parties into the United Nicaraguan Opposition coalition (UNO) (Robinson 1992, 52–53). Rumors circulated in Managua that the United States would spend more than $45 million in covert funding to the opposition. The United States would eventually publicly spend $12.5 million through the NED on the Nicaraguan election (HI 1989b). However, some observers point out that if one includes covert and circuitous spending, the real figure approaches $30 million (Robinson 1992, 62). The administration also helped select and fund a charismatic opposition presidential candidate, newspaper publisher Violeta Barrios de Chamorro. Violeta Chamorro was an extremely attractive candidate. The widow of national hero Pedro Joaquín Chamorro and a member of the first revolutionary junta, Doña Violeta had impeccable anti-Somoza credentials. Similarly, as publisher of the antigovernment newspaper *La Prensa* and given her early resignation from the revolutionary junta in 1980 because of the government's leftward drift, she was also a veteran of the anti-Sandinista opposition. Moreover, Chamorro's personal life seemed to symbolize Nicaragua's internal divisions, as two of her children had joined her in opposition while two others were Sandinistas. Furthermore, Chamorro was viewed by many Nicaraguans as a potential candidate of national reconciliation.

The Bush administration originally wanted Congress to waive the prohibition against using the National Endowment for Democracy to support a particular candidate or party in order to ensure that the endowment could help UNO. The administration's proposal included $3 million in overt aid to UNO for the election. Assistant Secretary of State Aronson described the proposal as "a modest program" to assist democratic forces in "a David versus Goliath fight" (quoted in Pear 1989, 9). Supporters of the proposal argued that the waiver would be appropriate because Nicaragua was a special case for the only "genuinely" democratic ticket in the running to have a chance; the democrats would need to overcome the advantages of a regime that dominated public debate while censuring and restricting opposition voices for most of the prior ten years (*New York Times*, September 14, 1989). Similarly, Antonio Lacayo, UNO's campaign director, argued that such an exemption would not be "a change in policy because the NED would not be giving money to a political party but to a cause that is essentially the cause of democracy" (quoted in Hockstader 1989, A14).

Congress balked at granting the waiver. Senator Christopher Dodd, chair-

the bipartisan agreement, the CIA phased out payments to the Miami-based contra directorate, and U.S. officials encouraged the contras to return home and support the political opposition. The CIA then began sending money under a new covert program called the Nicaraguan Exile Relocation program, ostensibly to cover the cost of relocating to Nicaragua. According to sources who have seen the CIA records, one of the recipients of the funds was Alfredo César, a former contra official who helped run Chamorro's presidential campaign (Marquis 1992). During the congressional debate on funding the Nicaraguan opposition, Senator Claiborne Pell asked Aronson if the administration was planning any "covert operations" to influence the Nicaraguan elections. At the time, Aronson declined to answer, saying such questions should be discussed behind closed doors by the congressional intelligence panels (Pear 1989).

The White House also acquired funding for the Nicaraguan opposition from third countries. At the United Nations, Secretary of State James Baker asked the foreign ministers of Japan and West Germany to request political parties in their countries to contribute funds to Chamorro's campaign. Baker made similar requests to other close U.S. allies, including conservative Arab regimes.

The decision of the Bush administration to meddle in the Nicaraguan elections distorted the campaign. United States aid to the Nicaraguan opposition became a major issue in the campaign and came to symbolize each party's approach to U.S.-Nicaraguan relations. The Sandinistas portrayed their domestic critics as puppets of U.S. imperialism and themselves as the true nationalists and the defenders of national sovereignty. Daniel Ortega, after the $9 million aid package was approved by the U.S. Congress, declared that he was not worried. He predicted that voters would reject UNO as "political mercenaries of the United States" (quoted in Boudreaux 1989, 8). Ortega derided Chamorro and her vice president as "nothing but instruments." He stated further, "My real opposition is the North American government. My latest adversary is named George Bush. He is the other candidate in Nicaragua. . . . I am ready to debate him in Washington or in Managua, or we can debate by satellite. . . . He knows what he wants so we can talk. With the others there is nothing to discuss" (Boudreaux 1989, 8). Ortega also made it clear that if elected he was not going to ask for U.S. economic aid. He said that U.S. aid was not necessary because after the election aid was certain to flow from Western Europe, Japan, and multilateral lending agencies such as the World Bank (Vanden and Walker 1991, 173).

On the other hand, Chamorro's campaign was aided by the promise to improve relations with the United States. Because of its close ties to the

and Honduras and pressured these societies to adopt a new political formula. The centerpiece of this new arrangement was the replacement of the old military-oligarchy alliance with a new partnership between the military and conservative elements in the middle class. The United States also used its military, political, and economic power to pressure the Sandinistas to adopt election laws, which permitted the Bush administration to organize and fund the Nicaraguan opposition. This new form of intervention could ultimately be counterproductive to both U.S. interests and democracy. The use of U.S. moneys and power to influence the electoral process in Nicaragua and the other Central American republics could have serious repercussions in the rest of the hemisphere. Latin leaders, especially nationalists of either the Right or Left, may ask themselves whether elections will serve as nothing more than a "respectable" weapon to remove regimes that the United States considers detrimental to its interests. The fear that external forces, specifically the United States, will manipulate the electoral process in Latin American societies could damage the credibility of the "democratic revolution" in Latin America.

Electoral intervention also poses serious problems for U.S. foreign policy. The democratic revolution, which the Reagan and Bush administrations described in such glowing terms, depends on a relatively narrow conception of democracy. Central American societies are still marred by human rights abuses, police violence, and the hegemony of the armed forces. Central American elections, while restoring some political and civil liberties, have not been mechanisms for structural reforms; rather, they have served as an instrument for the removal of governments and politicians who were opposed to the status quo or no longer capable of preserving it. The recent wave of political violence in Venezuela, Peru, and Colombia illustrates that democratic regimes are not immune from instability. Elections, in order to forestall revolutionary violence, must be mechanisms for social and economic change as well as political change.

Electoral intervention in Central America in the 1980s has served U.S. security and economic interests far more than the cause of democracy. Critics of the United States have argued that this shows that U.S. foreign policy is still predicated on intervention, hegemony, and the arrogance of empire. However, while most of the rhetoric in support of democracy was disingenuous, the prodemocracy policy did serve to reduce the level of violence in Central America. In both El Salvador and Nicaragua the United States was forced to accept, after a decade of bitter civil war, the legitimacy of leftist movements. The prodemocracy policy of the United States has many serious flaws, but it did provide the United States with an alternative to the anti-Communist

America, edited by John A. Booth and Mitchell A. Seligson, 40–59. Chapel Hill: University of North Carolina Press.

Salomón, Leticia. 1984. "La doctrina de la seguridad nacional en Honduras." *Honduras boletín informativo* (Tegucigalpa: Centro de Documentación de Honduras) (May).

Selser, Gregoria. 1982. *Honduras: República alquilada*. Coyoacán, Mexico: Mex Sur.

Shepherd, Philip. 1986. "Honduras." In *Confronting Revolution: Security through Diplomacy in Central America*, edited by Morris J. Blachman, William M. LeoGrande, and Kenneth Sharpe, 125–55. New York: Pantheon.

Tulchin, Joseph S., and Knut Walter. 1991. "Nicaragua: The Limit of Intervention." In *Exporting Democracy: The United States and Latin America: Case Studies*, vol. 2, edited by Abraham F. Lowenthal, 111–41. Baltimore: Johns Hopkins University Press.

Vance, Cyrus. 1979. Address to the Foreign Policy Association. New York City, September 27.

Vanden, Harry E., and Thomas W. Walker. 1991. "The Reimposition of U.S. Hegemony over Nicaragua." In *Understanding the Central American Crisis*, edited by Kenneth Coleman and George Herring, 153–77. Wilmington, Del.: Scholarly Resource Books.

Wiarda, Howard. 1988. "Can Democracy Be Exported? The Quest for Democracy in U.S. Latin America Policy." In *The United States and Latin America in the 1980s*, edited by Kevin Middlebrook and Carlos Rico, 325–52. Pittsburgh: University of Pittsburgh Press.

would be those, at any given time, who are relatively less constrained by structure and have relatively more scope for action. Eliteness must be seen as relative.

Elites in the Central American Political Tradition

The central feature of political organization in Central America since colonial times has been clientelism, an unequal exchange whereby weaker clients provide support to stronger patrons, in return for protection and security.[2] Nineteenth-century caudillos throughout Central America built their power on pyramids of patron-client relationships. The traditional Liberal and Conservative Parties that emerged throughout the region were essentially rival coalitions of patrons, each with a clientele whose votes and machetes could be delivered.

Force was the principal means of changing a regime. Constitutions were helpful to international respectability, and elections were held regularly. However, elections were normally controlled and served only to legitimate the party or faction in power. To remove these incumbents usually required the use of force, and that was the substance of most of Central America's civil wars in the nineteenth century. The political process was essentially a zero-sum game between ins and outs, in which those who controlled the government would use its resources to entrench themselves in power and to enhance their wealth. Those on the outside knew they would never be permitted to win an election and that they would have to seize power by force if they wanted access to its benefits.[3]

The early twentieth century saw substantial political differentiation among the Central American countries, even as their insertion into the international economy was increasingly similar, based on agricultural exports (Cardoso and Pérez Brignoli 1977). Panama and Nicaragua had the misfortune, as potential canal sites, to attract the attention of the United States, and their political evolution has never really escaped that influence, derived from prolonged U.S. military presence and political intervention, added to the profound economic penetration that these two countries shared with the rest of the isthmus. Although the United States certainly did not control all details of the political evolution in these countries, it may at least be affirmed that no one held political power for very long in either country against the will of the U.S. government, until the rise of the Sandinistas in 1979.[4]

Depression and Rumors of War

The Great Depression and World War II put great strains on all the political systems of Central America, tending to promote mobilization of new mass publics, to put new political and economic issues on the agenda, and to fragment political elites.[5] Everywhere, there was substantial success in organizing both rural and urban workers, whose demands for higher wages, social benefits, and better working conditions forced political elites to pay attention. The emergence of Communist parties (at least theoretically revolutionary) throughout the region in the early 1930s lent a special militance to these organizing efforts and a particular urgency to elite attempts to respond to the new demands. A growing urban middle class was less amenable to organization than the workers but shared many of the same grievances, as well as being particularly concerned with issues of individual liberty and political democracy. The adherence of all of Central America to the Allied cause of defending democracy against totalitarianism in World War II thus posed potentially mortal threats to the legitimacy of the authoritarian governments. Finally, the wartime alliance of the United States with the Soviet Union shifted international parameters in favor of Communist support for incumbent governments, a configuration that rather suddenly went out of fashion again in the late 1940s with the advent of the cold war.

Where military dictators were entrenched, in Guatemala, Honduras, and Nicaragua, these broad international changes elicited delayed responses, ranging from the overthrow of Jorge Ubico in Guatemala in 1944, and of Tiburcio Carías Andino in Honduras in 1948, to the survival of the Somoza regime in Nicaragua. A reformist regime in Guatemala was overthrown with CIA aid in 1954 (Immerman 1982; Schlesinger and Kinzer 1982), giving way to a generation of rightist military regimes. The basic reality of military domination in all three countries would not be challenged again until the 1980s.

The crisis of depression and war had a more immediate and profound effect on the civil oligarchies in El Salvador, Panama, and Costa Rica than in the three countries where dictators were entrenched. In El Salvador the challenge of a militant peasants' union led by Communists led the oligarchy to invite draconian military intervention by the army commander, Maximiliano Hernández Martínez, who seized power in 1931, and in the next year preempted an alleged uprising by ordering the slaughter of tens of thousands of peasants, including, of course, the union leadership (Anderson 1971). Hernández Martínez ruled until 1944, but the armed forces remained in direct control of the government through several coups and numerous elections,

pact also entailed acceptance by both sides of their respective rights to govern, to carry out distinct policy commitments, and of their obligation, in governing, to respect the vital interests of their opponent and counterpart. The pact constituted the democratic regime, becoming its anchor. As the stability of the regime became evident, the forces excluded from it (*calderonistas* and the Left) accepted it and were accepted as political participants under its terms (Peeler 1992).

Such pacts are important to the foundation of democracies because the practice of democracy demands a level of trust among rival elites that is rarely, if ever, found outside democratic regimes.[6] Procedurally, democracy entails a willingness on the part of a government voluntarily to yield power if it loses an election and to nevertheless assure that such an election is honestly held. Correspondingly, democracy entails a willingness on the part of the opposition to eschew violent assaults on the government, waiting instead for periodic elections as the only acceptable means of displacing the government. The difficulty of these stipulations is enhanced by the likelihood that substantive policies of government and opposition will differ in important ways, so that who controls the government really matters, not only in terms of the spoils of office, but also in terms of real consequences for society. Under these circumstances, rival elites have little reason to support a democratic transition unless they can be satisfied that their most central interests will be respected. The key, at least in Costa Rica, was that rival elites became convinced that a properly safeguarded democracy might better serve their interests than a continuation of politics as usual, with all the costs and risks entailed.

Dictatorships and Transitions to Democracy

Each of the countries of the region, other than Costa Rica, has undergone substantial political changes since the late 1970s, including the establishment of liberal democratic regimes. Yet in no case does there appear to be a clear prospect of consolidating a stable democracy. Rather, in each case the emergence of democracy is largely the result of the conjuncture of international and internal conditions; when that conjuncture changes, we may expect regime changes as well.

Three countries—Nicaragua, El Salvador, and Guatemala—have undergone revolutionary upheavals in which entrenched and authoritarian regimes, representing economic elites and with little popular support, were challenged by counterelites with revolutionary socialist programs. All three were military dictatorships transparently masquerading as constitutional gov-

the Salvadoran regime, enabling it to parry every thrust of the FMLN, even though corruption, repression, and incompetence prevented them from winning outright.

Guatemala's experience has been even less like Nicaragua's. The URNG, the analogue of the FMLN and FSLN, has been able to maintain itself and to inflict damage, but by no stretch of the imagination has it threatened to take power. The armed forces and economic elite were essentially united on a counterinsurgency strategy that involved massive repression against the indigenous population. The mass of nonelite ladinos remained largely unmobilized. The Reagan administration sympathized with the counterinsurgency program but never committed large amounts of aid to Guatemala. The threat, however, was not so large that it could not be contained by a determined regime.

In both Guatemala and El Salvador, then, the emergence of formally democratic regimes in the 1980s must be seen in the context of internal and international struggles against revolutionary movements. From an internal perspective, the use of elections was very much in the Central American tradition, as a means of legitimating the ruling coalition. Competition was restricted to sectors that were acceptable to the armed forces and economic elites, because they did not propose fundamental redistribution of property and would not interfere with the armed forces and their counterinsurgency by terrorism. The insurgents and their supporters were systematically excluded from electoral competition (Herman and Brodhead 1984).

Nicaragua in the 1980s represents in many ways a mirror image of the Salvadoran case. The regime sought to lay the foundations for a revolutionary transformation of society, against the sustained, multifaceted opposition of the United States. The FSLN, uniquely among Marxist revolutionary movements, did not seek to establish a single-party dictatorship but rather a revolutionary counterpart of the typical bourgeois democracy, wherein revolutionaries, rather than bourgeois parties, would set the rules and win most elections while tolerating minority parties representing bourgeois interests, so long as the latter accepted the revolutionary rules of the game (Coraggio 1986; Ruchwarger 1987). Major emphasis was placed on organization and mobilization of the population through neighborhood revolutionary defense committees and organizations of peasants, workers, and women. Basic Christian communities growing out of the "popular church" movement within the Catholic Church and similar organizations within Protestant denominations also provided important support for the revolutionary regime. Against this revolutionary coalition, anti-Somoza sectors of the bourgeoisie and the Catholic hierarchy moved rather quickly to join exiled Somoza partisans and other members of

their own supporters of betraying their causes. As yet there is no assurance that the Nicaraguans have laid the foundation for a durable democratic regime.

Bush's willingness to accept a Sandinista role in the Chamorro government was a manifestation of a general political shift on a world scale that has shifted the parameters not only for Nicaragua but also for El Salvador and Guatemala. The fall of Communist regimes in Eastern Europe and the Soviet Union and the consequent end of the cold war have withdrawn the external support for ongoing conflicts in these countries. In Nicaragua the Sandinistas can no longer rely on significant support from either the Soviet Union or Cuba. On the other hand, the Bush administration showed a will to relegate Central America to its accustomed lowly place in U.S. foreign policy, after a decade of unusual attention. Moreover, the massive U.S. budget deficit has curtailed the ability of any administration to deliver substantial aid, even were it so inclined. Thus, at a minimum, external circumstances emphatically favor reducing the intensity of conflicts and permit such initiatives as the Chamorro-Sandinista entente.

El Salvador has felt the effects of the same external changes. During 1991 and 1992, long-standing negotiations between the government and the FMLN finally began to show progress, culminating in a U.N.-brokered agreement that committed the FMLN to disarmament, in return for its incorporation into civil politics as a political party. The government, in turn, committed itself to disband the special forces responsible for most human rights violations, to halve the size of the armed forces, to create a new civil police force to which former guerrillas might belong, and to revise training for the armed forces to eliminate doctrines that have promoted human rights violations and military seizure of political power.

The Salvadoran agreement of 1992 is another potential elite settlement. The key question concerns the response of the armed forces: if the high command comes to see that the institution's interests will be as well or better protected under the agreement than if it continued the war with declining external support, it may adhere to the agreement. Even then, it may not be able to hold lower-ranking officers in line. But there is at least the possibility that 1992 might mark a turning point for El Salvador, the successful incorporation of the Left into a democratic political system with civilian control of the armed forces. The successful completion of the 1994 elections are a good sign.

Similar negotiations between the URNG and the government have been under way in Guatemala, but without definitive progress. The URNG is in a much weaker position than the FMLN but is subject to the same loss of external support. On the other hand, the armed forces are relatively stronger than their

power until the United States weighed in. Confronting the Sandinistas in Nicaragua, and trying to bolster the regime in El Salvador, neither Carter nor Reagan was inclined to tolerate a highly visible petty dictator in Honduras. The Honduran armed forces acceded to the pressure but remained in the background as the decision makers of last resort within the country. Particularly under President Roberto Suazo Córdoba (1981–86), the armed forces commander, Gustavo Alvarez Martínez, was immune from presidential control and worked closely with the United States to make Honduras the logistical keystone of Reagan policy in Central America.

Prior to this unusual U.S. government interest in Honduras, the normal political pattern in recent decades orbited around the elites of the two traditional parties (National and Liberal), one of which (most often the Nationals) would establish a self-perpetuating hegemony in alliance with the armed forces (Morris 1984; Rosenberg 1990). The election of two consecutive Liberals in the 1980s was a break in a long National Party–armed forces alliance. It now appears that the armed forces are willing to work with either of the major parties, though tensions were emerging with the newly elected Liberal president, Carlos Roberto Reina, in 1994.

As the attention and resources of the United States are steadily diverted from Central America, the Honduran democracy will be quite vulnerable to a military takeover. While the United States provided large amounts of aid during the 1980s, little was done to rectify the structural problems of poverty and underdevelopment. Consequently, the mass of the population, while not revolutionary, has little reason to defend the regime. Meanwhile, the major party elites have not shown the sort of vision and commitment that would lead political rivals to collaborate in maintaining the democratic regime. On the contrary, the most likely outcome will be a reversion to Honduran politics as usual, with one of the parties ruling in an authoritarian alliance with the armed forces.

Panama, paradoxically, was allowed to resist the pressure for democratization during the 1980s, in large part because its military ruler after 1981, Manuel Noriega, was useful to the United States as an intelligence source on both the Sandinistas and the Castro regime in Cuba. His notorious corruption and drug trafficking were tolerated and kept quiet by the U.S. government until, with the end of the cold war and the weakening of both Cuba and Nicaragua, he could be dispensed with through the invasion of December 1989. The civilian political elite, based fundamentally in the commercial-industrial class of Panama City and Colón, had always been fragmented and had been seriously weakened by the populist reforms of Noriega's military predecessor, Omar Torrijos (1968–81). They could not pose an independent challenge to

glect, hostility, or control. Neglect is the normal mode, when the United States pays little attention to the region, and Central Americans are left to their own devices and resources. If the U.S. government perceives the government of a Central American country as seriously threatening its interests, the historical response has normally been to seek that government's removal by indirect (e.g., Nicaragua, 1981–90) or direct (e.g., Panama, 1989) means. If a Central American government is seen by the United States as friendly (at a time when the United States is paying attention to Central America), the United States will tend to exercise broad political control over that country (e.g., El Salvador and Honduras in the 1980s).

The dominant Costa Rican elites have generally shown an understanding of how to maximize their scope for autonomous action relative to the United States. Costa Rican foreign policy is consistently pro-American, regardless of the party in power, and every Costa Rican government since 1948 has been anti-Communist. The Costa Rican commitment to democracy is a prominent feature of the country's self-image and is stated in liberal terms that are congenial to U.S. ears. The relatively strong Costa Rican state has generally been administered with reasonable efficiency, and the economy has been managed to avoid the worst pitfalls such as hyperinflation. This overall history of prudent competence has afforded the leading Costa Rican elites enough maneuvering room to maintain the strong welfare state and state control of banking and insurance, even though these features are in some tension with U.S. conventional wisdom.

The emergence of the Third World debt crisis in the early 1980s increased Costa Rica's dependence on U.S. aid and vulnerability to U.S. pressure, as the country, like many others, found itself unable to service its debt.[15] At the same time, the escalation of the U.S. confrontation with the Sandinistas made Washington pay more attention to the region and rendered Costa Rica, as Nicaragua's southern neighbor, strategically important. The result was that Costa Rica got more aid than it might otherwise have gotten, cushioning the effects of the debt crisis. The government of Luis Alberto Monge (PLN, 1982–86) proved highly amenable to these pressures; Monge's successor, Oscar Arias (PLN, 1986–90), was more resistant. The Arias government resisted U.S. strategic pressure on two fronts, internal and external. Internally, shady operations resulting from Monge's concessions were exposed and treated as in conflict with Costa Rica's constitution or with its neutral and peaceful foreign policy. Externally, the principal strategy of Arias aimed for an autonomous Central American peace settlement, which was finally concluded in 1987 after the United States had been diplomatically outmaneuvered (Rojas and Solís 1988; Child 1992; Moreno 1994). The diplomacy of the Arias Peace Plan

nosis is extremely troubled. The coalition installed in power by U.S. bayonets has fallen apart, the attempt of the Endara government to abolish the Panama Defense Force has been blocked by a popular referendum, and the old Torrijos party regained power in elections in 1994.

Can Costa Rica maintain the democracy it has? Probably, because the Costa Rican elites have proved astute in navigating hazardous waters. Will the rest of Central America and Panama achieve the benefits of stable democracy in the foreseeable future? Probably not, because of a whole array of structural constraints previously discussed. The most powerful Central American elites (armed forces and bourgeoisie) have largely lacked the imagination to see how politics could be different, and they have lacked the political skill to find ways of mitigating the constraints, by either interelite cooperation or mass mobilization.

While most of Central America will be lucky to keep the precarious liberal democracies it has, there is the potential in Costa Rica for carrying democracy to a new level, for "deepening" democracy (Peeler 1990). A widespread critique of liberal democracy (summarized by Booth in the introduction) holds that it cannot approach its aspiration of true equality of political power without doing more to reduce economic inequalities,[16] which are almost as extreme in Costa Rica as they are in the rest of Central America. This argument can be made at the level of right: that political equality can only be meaningful to the extent that economic inequality does not give a rich individual more power than a poor one. A society of perfect equality is obviously an unattainable ideal, but it would not be unreasonable to aim at a distribution of income similar to that of Sweden or the Netherlands, for example, which would raise the proportion of income received by the lowest 20 percent from 4 percent to around 8 percent, while lowering the proportion received by the top 10 percent from 34.1 percent to around 20 percent (World Bank 1994, 220–21, table 30).

The argument can also be made at the level of prudence. Allowing the poorer part of the population more resources can be expected to reduce social tensions and enhance stability, to promote positive trends in other aspects of human development such as health and education, and to increase the size of the internal market. Moreover, a more egalitarian society need not undermine economic growth: Japan and the four more recent economic dynamos of East Asia (South Korea, Hong Kong, Taiwan, and Singapore) have much more egalitarian income distributions than Costa Rica or any other Latin American country.[17]

The dominant political elites of Costa Rica have a consistent record of having the sort of enlightened grasp of their own self-interest that could lead them into such a program of moderate economic and social democratization.

10. Again, the literature is voluminous. See especially Walker (1987), Schoultz (1986), and Tulchin and Walter (1991).

11. For most of Reagan's term, such covert support of the contras was prohibited by Congress but was carried out anyway. When this became undeniable after the Sandinistas downed a CIA plane, the "Iran-contra" scandal developed. See Moyers (1988).

12. A good running narrative of Central American affairs since 1989 can be found in issues of the *Latin American Weekly Report* and *Latin American Regional Report*.

13. Suzanne Jonas, writing in this volume, argues that the political will for a settlement is, indeed, emerging in Guatemala.

14. The exception is Panama, which depends fundamentally on the canal, not agriculture, for foreign exchange.

15. The Third World debt crisis was caused fundamentally by the sudden rise in world petroleum prices in the late 1970s, covered by extensive Third World borrowing from commercial banks. See Stallings and Kaufman (1989). Costa Rica's situation was exacerbated by the unusual incompetence of the Carazo government (1978–82). See Trejos S. (1985) and Duncan (1989).

16. See, for example, Macpherson (1973).

17. This argument is made at greater length, for Latin America as a whole, in Peeler (1990). Cf. Jaguaribe et al. (1986). The data in United Nations Development Program (1991) show that, on a wide range of measures of human well-being, more democratic countries are also better off in terms of human development. It should be acknowledged, though, that many countries with very low per capita GNP also have egalitarian income distributions (e.g., India, Bangladesh). Part of the explanation for persistent extreme inequality in Latin America probably includes a long tradition of predatory class relations, a tradition simply encouraged by liberal economic doctrines of the last two centuries, which have undermined traditional paternalism.

References

Anderson, Thomas P. 1971. *Matanza: El Salvador's Communist Revolt of 1932*. Lincoln: University of Nebraska Press.

Baloyra, Enrique. 1982. *El Salvador in Transition*. Chapel Hill: University of North Carolina Press.

Booth, John A. 1985. *The End and the Beginning*. 2d ed. Boulder, Colo.: Westview Press.

Booth, John A., and Mitchell A. Seligson, eds. 1989. *Elections and Democracy in Central America*. Chapel Hill: University of North Carolina Press.

Brockett, Charles D. 1990. *Land, Power, and Poverty*. Boston: Unwin Hyman.

Bulmer-Thomas, Victor. 1987. *The Political Economy of Central America since 1920*. Cambridge: Cambridge University Press.

Burton, Michael, Richard Gunther, and John Higley. 1992. "Introduction: Elites, Transformations, and Democratic Regimes." In *Elites and Democratic Consolidation in Latin America and Southern Europe*, edited by John Higley and Richard Gunther, 1–37. Cambridge: Cambridge University Press.

Calvert, Peter. 1985. *Guatemala: A Nation in Turmoil*. Boulder, Colo.: Westview Press.

Cardoso, Ciro F. X., and Héctor Pérez Brignoli. 1977. *Centroamérica y la economía occidental, 1520–1930*. San José, Costa Rica: Editorial Universidad de Costa Rica.

Child, Jack. 1992. *The Central American Peace Process, 1983–1991*. Boulder, Colo.: Lynne Rienner.

Coraggio, José Luis. 1986. *Nicaragua: Revolution and Democracy*. Boston: Allen and Unwin.

Duncan, Cameron. 1989. "Costa Rica: Conditionality and the Adjustment Policies of USAID in the Eighties." Paper presented at the Latin American Studies Association, Miami, December.

——. 1986. *National Security and United States Policy toward Latin America*. Princeton: Princeton University Press.

Stallings, Barbara, and Robert Kaufman, eds. 1989. *Debt and Democracy in Latin America*. Boulder, Colo.: Westview Press.

Trejos S., Juan Diego. 1985. *Costa Rica: Economic Crisis and Public Policy*. Occasional Paper No. 11. Miami: Florida International University.

Tulchin, Joseph, and Knut Walter. 1991. "Nicaragua: The Limits of Intervention." In *Exporting Democracy: The United States and Latin America*, 2 vols., edited by Abraham F. Lowenthal, 2:111–41. Baltimore: Johns Hopkins University Press.

United Nations Development Program. 1991. *Human Development Report*. New York: Oxford University Press.

Vega C., José Luis. 1982. *Poder político y democracia en Costa Rica*. San José, Costa Rica: Editorial Porvenir.

Walker, Thomas W. 1987. *Reagan versus the Sandinistas: The Undeclared War*. Boulder, Colo.: Westview Press.

——, ed. 1986. *Nicaragua: The First Five Years*. New York: Praeger.

——. 1991. *Revolution and Counterrevolution in Nicaragua*. Boulder, Colo.: Westview Press.

Wiarda, Howard, and Harvey Kline, eds. 1990. *Latin American Politics and Development*. 3d ed. Boulder, Colo.: Westview Press.

Williams, Robert G. 1986. *Export Agriculture and the Crisis in Central America*. Chapel Hill: University of North Carolina Press.

Woodward, Ralph Lee. 1976. *Central America: A Nation Divided*. New York: Oxford University Press.

World Bank. 1994. *World Development Report*. New York: Oxford University Press.

We now know that Central Americans, despite the relative brevity of their experience as citizens of electoral democracies, act very much like citizens of other nations—they participate in politics in patterns and at levels like those observed in industrial democracies (Booth and Richard 1994). In the early 1990s, report Seligson et al. in Chapter 7, there was little difference among the correlates and predictors of registration, voting, and abstention in Central America from those observed elsewhere.

Of course there remain marked differences among the six nations in certain institutions, political cohesion, and their consolidation of liberal democracy.[1] However, that such similar regimes have emerged from national experiences so diverse as revolution and counterrevolution, insurrection and stagnated civil war, reformist military populism, military devolution of power to civilians, and imposition by an external power suggests that certain powerful constraints have shaped both the form and substance of Central American democratization.

External Constraints Favoring Democracy

Aside from fair elections themselves, the greatest novelty of the Central American political scene by 1990 was geopolitical. Peeler and Moreno, in their chapters, emphasize the changes in the international context within which the Central American polities and elites have operated. At the beginning of the 1980s the cold war kept containment of communism at the top of the U.S. policy agenda and left democratization the stepchild of U.S. interests. However, a combination of public and congressional opposition to armed intervention eventually forced the Reagan administration to promote human rights and an electoralist version of democracy in Central America as prerequisites for continued congressional funding of containment in El Salvador and Nicaragua. With the evaporation of the cold war, the Bush administration elevated hemispheric democratization to a more central goal from its formerly contingent status. As the 1980s unfolded, the United States increasingly pressured key elites, especially the armed forces, to abandon military authoritarianism and to develop and respect systems of civilian, constitutional, electoral politics with improved human rights.

Other international pressures in favor of democracy also developed. First, during the 1970s and 1980s the Organization of American States, the United Nations, the Roman Catholic Church, the European Community, and numerous European and Latin American nations labored on many different fronts to promote democracy in Central America. They sought democracy for

vote and voting are the most widespread activities. From 74 to 94 percent of urbanites reported being registered, and from 56 to 89 percent reported voting. Communal activism is the next most common type, followed in descending order by organizational activity, electioneering, and contacting public officials. Participation levels tend to be highest in Honduras and Panama and much lower in El Salvador and Guatemala (table C.1).[4]

These patterns clearly indicate that breadth of participation in Central America tends to be greater where levels of political turmoil, violence, and rebellion are lower. Indeed, with all the samples pooled, multiple regression reveals that a structural measure of repression ranking the Central American nations in order of political repressiveness was the most powerful predictor of participation levels when analyzed in conjunction with several socioeconomic, resource, and attitudinal variables.[5] Greater repression lowered almost all forms of citizen activism. Moreover, a psychological measure of perceived repression also correlated strongly with lower levels of participation among Central Americans (Booth 1992; Booth and Richard 1994).

The Development of Democratic Culture

Do elections contribute to a political culture of support for participation and democratic rules of the game? It is, of course, difficult to determine the direction of causal influence between institutions and political culture—that is, whether institutions determine culture or vice versa.[6] Nevertheless, as noted in the introduction to this volume, many observers have expressed doubt that Latin Americans, especially in authoritarian (or only newly democratized) settings are prone to support democratic liberties. Are Central Americans authoritarian, or are they democratically inclined?

The same public opinion surveys cited above provide some recent evidence about support for democratic norms among contemporary Central American urban dwellers. This study examined fourteen variables indicating support for civil liberties. They were factor analyzed for possible patterns of covariation among them, and four distinct clusters of attitudes were found and combined into indices (table C.2). National-level attitudes toward civil liberties varied notably in urban Central America in the early 1990s; the differences in means tests for all indices in table C.2 are significant at the .001 level or better.

Most interesting is that, these differences notwithstanding, Central Americans support most democratic liberties. Table C.2 reveals first that support for general participation rights (GENRIGHT) averaged 7.89 on the 10-point scale, support for dissenters' rights (RIGHTDIS) averaged 5.93, and opposition to the suppression of democratic liberties (OSDL) averaged 6.10—all firmly in the positive end of the scale. Overall, Guatemalans and Salvadorans manifested the lowest support (but still strongly supportive of participatory rights) and Panamanians and Hondurans the highest. Guatemala was particularly low, however, in support for the right to dissent. Only on the item of support for civil disobedience (CIVILDIS) did Central Americans on average give negative responses (the mean is only 2.35). Clearly such actions as blocking streets, invading property, or attempting to overthrow the government were not generally acceptable among urban Central Americans. Other studies of these data have revealed that repression lowers urban Central Americans' support for civil liberties but has a less dampening effect on democratic culture than on participation levels (Booth 1992, 20; Booth and Richard 1994).

Election Quality and the Depth of Democracy

In several Central American nations the improvement in the probity of elections has increased the depth of political participation. Elections had often been fraudulently manipulated or held under conditions unfair to some competitors and to the electorate. Elections becoming increasingly free and generally fair in Central America over the last decade has deepened democracy by letting citizens express their true preferences in leadership contests without intimidation, having their votes honestly counted, and implementing the results.

The opening of space for political participation, both electoral and otherwise, has perhaps also somewhat deepened democracy in Central America. Electoral democratization and the accompanying improvement in human rights performance have made it possible for citizens to associate more freely, mobilize to pursue their interests, petition the government, and obtain and exchange information. The resultant expansion of civil society represents a true deepening of democracy. To some extent this expansion of political space has been abetted early on by international pressures and sometimes by the presence of international election observers. Ultimately, however, the long-term consolidation of democracy in the region will depend much more on institutionalizing elite respect for democratic rules and participatory rights than it will on pressure or intervention by external agents.

Elite Settlements and Regime Consolidation

A widely held agreement among key elites to play by democratic rules, to tolerate one another, and to accept as legitimate participation by mass publics

onduras (696)	El Salvador (696)	Nicaragua (673)	Panama (695)
8.07	7.47	8.32	8.46
6.99	5.21	5.69	7.10
5.82	5.25	6.45	6.78
3.41	2.12	2.42	1.96
6.46	5.01	5.72	6.08

[a]The Costa Rican sample did not include the items from which this index was constructed.
[b]Note that this item is couched positively, so that—like the other three indexes—a high score represents support for civil liberties.
[c]This index is an unweighted average of the other four indexes.

many following World War II and developed and consolidated itself over time in formerly authoritarian settings in southern Europe. Something similar might well eventually occur in Central America. Cold-war paranoia about mass participation in politics and left parties has diminished among power elites both in Washington and in the isthmus. Because such fears have often driven the antidemocratic behavior of the Right in Central America, the waning of these fears gives supporters of democracy some cause for hope. Moreover, the objectives and techniques of the Left have moderated greatly in recent years. Should conservative regional elites observe that their societies can function in an electoral mode that allows space for civil society without the long-feared social chaos and revolution, they may begin to accommodate one another and come to peace with democracy.

An Overview of the Region

Based on the foregoing, one should obviously not conclude that either the election of civilian governments in Central American nations or even the passing of power to victorious opponents means that democracy has become consolidated in the isthmus. On the other hand, if democracy means par-

governmental promotion of certain types of popular participation through the formation of nongovernmental organizations.

Honest elections in a climate of extensive political freedom for individuals, parties, most voluntary associations, and the press have been among Costa Rica's greatest achievements for four decades. Voters have developed a taste for alternating their ruling party; they have elected the PLN to power several times since the 1950s and various conservative opposition coalitions several times. There clearly exist both an elite and a mass consensus in favor of democracy that have weathered unscathed some difficult periods of economic strife (Seligson and Gómez B. 1989; Carvajal Herrera 1978). In comparative terms the breadth of Costa Rican political participation appears extensive and the range of participation is moderate (owing to the mixed economy and government mobilization of groups), but overall the depth of participation is rather modest.

In the 1980s, under Reagan and Bush administration and international lenders' neoliberal pressures during Costa Rica's post-1981 debt crisis, the country curtailed its social welfare policies and reduced state involvement in the economy. Such changes have somewhat reduced the range of political participation but have not seriously eroded support for the regime. Successful U.S. pressure to increase the size and strength of Costa Rica's security forces in cooperation with American policies against Nicaragua aroused fears of possible military intervention in politics. External pressures that have undercut constitutional norms and international neutrality, the presence of large numbers of anti-Sandinista rebels until 1990, increased paramilitary activity, and increased antileftist propaganda in Costa Rica have all contributed to some erosion of the government's respect for human rights in recent years, but no crisis has ensued.

El Salvador

Centuries of profound economic inequality and racist exploitation of Indian and mestizo poor by a socioeconomic elite descended from the conquerors bequeathed densely populated modern El Salvador severe problems of economic and social inequity. Popular demands for redress of various problems have periodically surfaced but have been regularly and violently repressed by the national bourgeoisie and the government. A brief reformist experiment in 1931 was quickly overthrown by the dictatorial General Hernández Martínez. When labor, peasant, and student groups assayed an abortive revolt in 1932, the dictator massacred thirty thousand people—mostly innocent peasants—and thus snuffed out for decades any inclination toward popular participation.

cause of the Central American peace process, which set in motion a gradual incorporation of the revolutionary Left into the electoral system. In new space purchased by the peace negotiations, the FDR contested the 1989 election, and following the 1992 peace accord the FMLN too became a legal political party and contested the 1994 election. The 1994 vote, conducted in an improved human rights climate, was marred by the apparent denial of voter registration to a substantial number of citizens of formerly FMLN-dominated areas and by the intimidation of groups working to register voters. These flaws probably cost the FMLN control of several municipal councils but would not have changed the outcome of the presidential race.

Did a new regime committed to democratic rules, mutual accommodation of major elite elements, and mass participation emerge from El Salvador's elections in the 1980s? Baloyra argues that 1980s Salvadoran votes have indeed contributed to the birth of a democratic political process. For both the populace and the nation's antagonistic and warring elites, elections have proved the sole viable alternative to perpetual warfare. Neither side in the civil war could win, so eventually elections became the only path out of a quagmire. The 1992 Salvadoran peace accord, albeit with several delays, has gradually been implemented. The army by 1994 had cut its forces by half to thirty-one thousand troops and grudgingly accepted the replacement and retirement of key officers. After being embarrassed by the discovery of hidden arms caches in 1993, by 1994 the FMLN had fully demobilized and largely converted itself into a political party (U.S. Dept. of State 1993).

Thus Salvadorans seem to have turned toward democratic electoral rules, but years of violence, repression, and intimidation and terror have profoundly shaped political values and behavior in El Salvador. Tables C.1 and C.2 demonstrate that, in comparison with other Central American countries' urban dwellers, the overall breadth of participation in El Salvador and support for democracy are comparatively limited, elections notwithstanding. A consolidation of this fledgling electoral democracy, improvement of human rights performance, and restoration of the rule of law may encourage Salvadorans to be more active in politics and support democratic liberties more strongly.

Guatemala

The northernmost and most populous of Central American states, Guatemala is roughly half Indian. Guatemala's socioeconomic history has been marked by exploitation of the indigenous populace's labor to benefit the creole and mestizo politico-economic elite. The nation's elites early developed pro-

atmosphere of extreme political repression that badly impeded communication. The Christian Democratic government of Marco Vinicio Cerezo Arévalo ruled with the advice and counsel of the military, which was exempted from prosecution for its past human rights abuses by the outgoing Mejía government and which retained virtually absolute control over military affairs. Cerezo's regime weathered at least two serious attempted coups but did finish its term.

Since the mid-1980s, in Guatemala City and other major cities, parties, unions, private associations, and development workers—once targets of fierce repression—have enjoyed expanded latitude for participation, expression of their opinions, and organization. In 1990 a new national election saw the discredited Christian Democrats lose the presidency to Jorge Serrano Elías, who invigorated peace talks between the government and the Guatemalan National Revolutionary Unity (Unidad Revolucionaria Nacional Guatemalteca—URNG) before being removed from office for the 1993 *autogolpe*. Politically motivated human rights abuses declined somewhat from pre-1985 levels, a national human rights ombudsman (Procuraduría de Derechos Humanos) was established, and a few a human rights violators from the security forces have been prosecuted since 1990. In rural areas, however, the massive military presence and control over the population and the counterinsurgency war against the URNG continued, severely depressing participation.

Political participation has increased somewhat in breadth and range under two successive civilian governments, but evidence as to its depth, efficacy, and staying power remains to be seen. Urban Guatemalans have among the lowest political participation rates and the lowest support for civil liberties in Central America (tables C.1 and C.2). Labor and peasant organizations have mobilized rapidly and have begun to test the range of their freedom. The tolerance of the armed forces for such participation is one key to the survival of civilian government. Another is the commitment of other elites to democracy. The 1993 *autogolpe* attempt by President Serrano revealed how tentative such commitment may be. Interestingly, under intense international pressure not to support the coup, the Guatemalan military backed away from Serrano and let the constitutional system replace him and narrowly rescue the democratic regime. The 1993 coup and Serrano's replacement by Ramiro de León Carpio demonstrated that most Guatemalan political activists, professionals, and some business leaders prefer democratic, participatory rules and increased political freedom. Given the depressing effect of historical, contemporary, and perceived repression on support for democratic norms (Booth and Richard 1994), public commitment to such rules and citizen participation in Guatemala will likely grow only as a function of diminished repression.

succeeded Suazo after another clean and fair election in 1986, followed in 1990 by the National Party's Rafael Callejas and in 1994 by Liberal Carlos Roberto Reina.

Has Honduras experienced a regime consolidation and truly democratizing elections since 1981? As Rosenberg argues in his chapter, five clean elections and four transfers of power constitute great progress in the consolidation of electoral democracy. Yet as he further notes, some political elites still lack commitment to accommodating one another and playing by democratic rules. As in Guatemala and El Salvador, the one absolutely critical elite is the military. The Honduran armed forces still have the capacity and quite possibly the will to intervene in politics should it seem convenient to key officers. One other threat to participation persists: political terror by public security forces. Although the death toll from political repression in Honduras since 1980 probably numbers only in the low hundreds in comparison with El Salvador's and Guatemala's tens of thousands, the menace to democracy is obvious.

Honduran mass political culture seems to be developing increased commitment to electoral and participatory rules under the Honduran civilian regimes of the 1980s, probably partly as a result of the extensive peasant and labor organization present in the country. There can be no doubt that the elections since 1980 have provided renewed opportunities for political participation that had been repressed in the previous decade. In 1991 urban political participation rates in Honduras (table C.1) were among the highest in the region, and support for democratic liberties (table C.2) was the highest.

Nicaragua

Nicaragua has suffered more civil war and foreign disruption of its affairs than almost any country in the hemisphere. The nineteenth and early twentieth centuries saw frequent Liberal-Conservative Party conflict, aggravated periodically by outside interference. American William Walker's 1855 invasion led to his expulsion in the National War of 1857 and to a three-decade period of Conservative Party rule. In the 1890s the Liberals returned to power, but the United States helped oust them in 1909 when they sought foreign suitors to build another transisthmian canal in Nicaragua. The United States then had to keep marines in Nicaragua for most of the next two decades, during which, in 1927, there arose an anti-intervention resistance movement led by Augusto C. Sandino. The United States escalated its military presence in Nicaragua and established a National Guard to help fight Sandino, but it eventually withdrew in frustration in 1933. Anastasio Somoza García, head of the National Guard, seized power and ruled as a dictator until his assassination in

Eventually President Ortega's government again restricted civil liberties, temporarily closed and regularly censored the principal opposition newspaper, and continued to defend the revolution militarily. Ultimately the regime could not keep the economy functioning adequately because of the war, and this undermined the Sandinista revolution's effort to promote broader, deeper, and a wider range of democracy through mass participation in policy making and implementation. As is common in revolution, popular mobilization and some regime elements were often intolerant of and intimidated opposition.

In February 1990 the Nicaraguan government conducted a new national election. Its rules were negotiated with the opposition, and massive external observation was arranged (Chapter 9). The FSLN renominated Daniel Ortega, who ran against Violeta Barrios de Chamorro, widow of former opposition publisher Pedro Joaquín Chamorro. She headed the twelve-party coalition known as the United Nicaraguan Opposition (Unión Nicaragüense Opositora—UNO), backed by the United States. Nicaragua's atrocious economy, anger at the government for the unpopular military draft, and hopes that, if UNO won, the war might end and the economy might improve all contributed to the FSLN's defeat. Giving the lie to many who believed that Marxists would never voluntarily relinquish power, President Ortega transferred power after successfully negotiating for the retention of a major FSLN presence in the army in order to prevent a rightist pogrom against the party.

Were the 1990 elections, transfer-of-power and contra demobilization negotiations, and later government-labor accords parts of a general interelite settlement in Nicaragua? Judging by the subsequent interelite conflict, one would have to say no. The United Nicaraguan Opposition broke apart into a centrist faction, headed by President Chamorro, and a rightist wing. Chamorro on occasion collaborates with the Sandinista legislative bench to pass legislation. Rightists have demanded the expulsion of the FSLN from the armed forces, denounced government collaboration with the Sandinistas, and even associated with disgruntled former contras, some of whom took up arms again in the early 1990s. However, despite these continuing difficulties, the 1990 vote constituted a major step toward democracy for Nicaragua because for the first time a powerful incumbent peacefully transferred power to a victorious opponent after conducting a clean election.

Popular participation in politics and support for democratic norms quite likely advanced under the Sandinista revolution. Table C.1 demonstrates that urban Nicaraguans are generally in the middle range of participation compared with their Central American counterparts, except for community self-

there has developed an elite settlement on democratic rules of the game remains to be seen. Endara's three-party coalition government broke up early in its term, but that does not necessarily mean a repudiation of democratic processes. The elimination for the short run of the Panamanian defense forces as a significant political actor and their anticipated political neutralization by U.S. forces based in Panama may help sustain a climate for elite consensus building.

In May 1994 Panama held its first free election since the fraud of 1989. Ernesto Pérez Balladares of the opposition Revolutionary Democratic Movement (Movimiento Revolucionario Democrático—MRD) won the election with only a third of the vote and assumed power without complications. These events clearly signify progress toward democratization, as did first civilian regime transfers of power to oppositions in each of the other isthmian nations. However, the factionalized and quarrelsome nature of the Panamanian political elite remains a problem for democratic consolidation.

Conclusions

Although Central America's six major nations now have elected civilian governments and constitutions providing for representative government and extensive participatory rights and civil liberties, one must not yet conclude that democratic regimes have been consolidated in the region.[9] Defining democracy as citizen participation in rule permits one to conclude, however, that recent elections have brought about or permitted real increases in the breadth and range of political participation to several countries. All the region's regimes have now experienced peaceful transfers of power to victorious opponents. There also appear to have been some efforts among elites to accommodate one another within electoral regimes, although the abortive coup by President Serrano in Guatemala reveals the potential frailty of elite commitment to democratic norms.

As a general proposition, it is obviously better for the advancement of democracy in Central America to have in power fairly elected civilian governments than to have dictatorial military governments. Even in the event of threatened coups, as in Guatemala, the persistence of constitutional, civilian government for multiple terms is a sign of progress toward democracy. However, such movement toward the requisites for effective and lasting democratic rule in the isthmus has been uneven and halting. International pressures for democracy, should they persist, may give time for democracy to consolidate, but important risk factors remain—especially elite discord, frail elite commit-

Seligson, Mitchell A., and Miguel Gómez B. 1989. "Ordinary Elections in Extraordinary Times." In *Elections and Democracy in Central America*, edited by John A. Booth and Mitchell A. Seligson, 158–84. Chapel Hill: University of North Carolina Press.

Smith, David A. 1992. "Panama: Political Parties, Social Crisis, and Democracy in the 1980s." In *Political Parties and Democracy in Central America*, edited by Louis W. Goodman, William M. LeoGrande, and Johanna Mendelson Forman, 213–33. Boulder, Colo.: Westview Press.

U.S. Department of State. 1993. "Report on Human Rights Practices in El Salvador." U.S. Embassy, San Salvador. Xerox.

Vilas, Carlos. 1994. "Democratización y gobernabilidad en un escenario post revolucionario: Centroamérica." Paper presented at the Ninth Congreso Centroamericano de Sociología, San Salvador, July 18–22.

Walker, Thomas W., ed. 1985. *Nicaragua: The First Five Years*. New York: Praeger.

NOTES ON THE CONTRIBUTORS

Leslie Anderson is associate professor of political science and affiliated with the Center for Latin American Studies at the University of Florida. Her research focuses on theories of peasant political action and on elections and democratic development in new democracies. Her work includes *The Political Ecology of the Modern Peasant* (1994) and numerous articles in political science journals. She is currently writing a book on the 1990 Nicaraguan election and has begun another comparing democratic development in Nicaragua and Argentina.

Enrique A. Baloyra-Herp is professor and director of Interamerican Studies of the Graduate School of International Studies, University of Miami. He is author of *El Salvador in Transition* (1982), coauthor (with John D. Martz) of *Political Attitudes in Venezuela* (1977), and coeditor (with James Morris) of *Conflict and Change in Cuba* (1993). His research has focused on democratization in Latin America, whether at the level of the masses (public opinion and voting behavior) or the elite (the politics of regime change).

John A. Booth is Regents Professor of Political Science at the University of North Texas. He is the author of *The End and the Beginning: The Nicaraguan Revolution* (1985), coauthor (with Thomas W. Walker) of *Understanding Central America* (1993), and coeditor (with Mitchell Seligson) of *Political Participation in Latin America*, Volumes 1 and 2 (1978 and 1979), and *Elections and Democracy in Central America* (1989). He continues research on and has published articles and essays on democracy, elections, revolution and political conflict, and U.S.-Central American relations.

Cynthia H. Chalker is a Ph.D. candidate in political science at the University of Pittsburgh. She is conducting her dissertation field research in Costa Rica on the political dynamics of structural adjustment. Her doctoral studies are supported by fellowships and grants from the Fulbright program, Inter-American Foundation, Tinker Foundation, and the Social Science Research Council.

Annabelle Conroy, a Bolivian national, is completing her doctoral dissertation at the University of Pittsburgh on the impact of local politics on national resource distribution in Bolivia. In 1995 she conducted dissertation field research with a fellowship from the Inter-American Foundation. She has published several papers, including one on context effects in Honduras in *Public Opinion Quarterly*, and completed a study of the legislature in El Salvador.

Margaret Scranton is professor of political science at the University of Arkansas at Little Rock. Author of *The Noriega Years: U.S.-Panamanian Relations, 1981–1990* (1991) and articles on Panamanian politics, she is currently working on a book on civilian opposition to Panama's military regime. Scranton has received research grants from the Fulbright-Hays Program, the United States Institute for Peace, and the Einstein Institute.

Mitchell A. Seligson is Daniel H. Wallace Professor of Political Science and research professor in the University Center for International Studies at the University of Pittsburgh. He has been studying Central America since the 1960s, when he served there as a U.S. Peace Corps volunteer. His most recent book is *Development and Underdevelopment: The Political Economy of Inequality*, edited with John Passè-Smith. His continuing research involves the political culture of democracy in Central America and a project on sustainable agriculture in the region.

Andrew J. Stein is a Ph.D. candidate in political science at the University of Pittsburgh. He holds master's degrees in Latin American studies and political science from New York University and the University of Pittsburgh. Stein conducted predissertation field work in Nicaragua in 1991 and returned there as a Fulbright fellow during 1993–94. He has written on electoral politics and religion and politics in Central America.

INDEX